# Dark Psychology:

*A Powerful Guide to Learn Persuasion, Psychological Warfare, Deception, Mind Control, Negotiation, NLP, Human Behavior and Manipulation! Great to Listen in a Car!*

# Table of contents

Introduction......5

Chapter one: The principles of dark psychology......7

Chapter two: "Dark personality" traits......16

Chapter three: Studies of dark psychology......39

Chapter four: Mind reading......52

Chapter five: Cognitive psychology......73

Chapter six: Modes of persuasion......97

Chapter seven: Controlling emotions......115

Chapter eight: Social engineering and leadership......127

Conclusion......140

© Copyright 2019 Tony Bennis - All rights reserved.

The following eBook is reproduced below with the goal of providing information that is as accurate and reliable as possible. Regardless, purchasing this eBook can be seen as consent to the fact that both the publisher and the author of this book are in no way experts on the topics discussed within and that any recommendations or suggestions that are made herein are for entertainment purposes only. Professionals should be consulted as needed prior to undertaking any of the action endorsed herein.

This declaration is deemed fair and valid by both the American Bar Association and the Committee of Publishers Association and is legally binding throughout the United States.

Furthermore, the transmission, duplication, or reproduction of any of the following work including specific information will be considered an illegal act irrespective of if it is done electronically or in print. This extends to creating a secondary or tertiary copy of the work or a recorded copy and is only allowed with an expressed written consent from the Publisher. All additional rights reserved.

The information in the following pages is broadly considered to be a truthful and accurate account of facts and as such any inattention, use, or misuse of the information in question by the reader will render any resulting actions solely under their purview. There are no scenarios in which the publisher or the original author of this work can be in any fashion deemed liable for any hardship or damages that may befall them after undertaking information described herein.

Additionally, the information in the following pages is intended only for informational purposes and should thus be thought of as universal. As befitting its nature, it is presented without assurance regarding its prolonged validity or interim quality. Trademarks that are mentioned are done without written consent and can in no way be considered an endorsement from the trademark holder

# Introduction

Congratulations on and thank you for downloading Dark Psychology. Here we will explore the more sordid and dark aspects of the human psyche, as well as some methods of applying our knowledge for use in our everyday lives. Here the following areas will be delved into the principles of dark psychology, "dark personality" traits, studies of dark psychology, mind reading, cognitive psychology, modes of persuasion, controlling emotions, and social engineering and leadership.

This book DOES NOT offer any formal health benefits and is intended for educational purposes only. Any health benefits or detriments associated with reading this book are merely circumstantial and coincidental. The writer does not condone using any information expressed here to better one's health.

Dark psychology accepts and embraces the darker side of the human experience. In this way it is doing the same as any area of anthropocentric study does, the only difference lying in dark psychology's specialty of this dark reality within the human animal. Dark psychology is not meant to be a pageant of villains, however. Specialists within this field do their work in order to better understand why and how malevolent people work toward their ends, not out of some attempt to gain fame for themselves and or to idolize the more monstrous among us. It is also important to keep in mind that each and every one of us has a dark or "evil" side of our own psychology. While there are some other conduits by which we can reach the realization of this side's contents, it is dark psychology that provides the clearest route for us in our way toward our enlightenment concerning how dark we truly are and why.

As you can tell, we have a lot of ground to cover within this book, so we should now dive on into our first subject regarding dark psychology: its principles.

# Chapter one: The principles of dark psychology

Dark psychology could best be described as a study of the human condition in which it becomes normative for people to pray upon others out of criminal and or deviant desires. Often these desires lack specific purpose and are based primarily on basic instinctual desires. Each human has the potential and capacity to victimize other humans, as well as other living creatures, but most of us keep these desires suppressed in order to function successfully in society. Those of us who do not sublimate these dark tendencies are typically representative of the "dark triad": psychopathy, sociopathy, and Machiavellianism, or other mental disorders/psychological disturbances. In this way, dark psychology focuses primarily on the underpinnings (i.e. the thoughts, processing systems, feelings, and behaviors) that are found below the more predatory aspects of our nature, the same ones that go most vigorously against the grain of modern thought concerning human behavior. In this field, we tend to assume that these more abusive, criminal, and deviant behaviors are purposive most of the time, though there are instances in which they seem to have no teleological underpinnings.

Dark psychology accepts and embraces the darker side of the human experience. In this way it is doing the same as any area of anthropocentric study does, the only difference lying in dark psychology's specialty of this dark reality within the human animal. Dark psychology is not meant to be a pageant of villains, however. Specialists within this field do their work in order to better understand why and how malevolent people work toward their ends, not out of some attempt to gain fame for themselves and or to idolize the more monstrous among us. It is also important to keep in mind that each and every one of us has a dark or "evil" side of our own psychology. While there are some other conduits by which we can reach the realization of this side's contents, it is dark psychology that provides the clearest route for us in our way toward our enlightenment concerning how dark we truly are and why.

Wrongdoing, as Socrates asserts, is doing that harms others. Not only does this harm others, but Socrates also thought that it harms our own souls, as many modern people would agree. Dark psychologists allow that some of us do wrong onto others for no greater purposes. Their ends never justify their means because there are simply no ends to be found. This capability (and perhaps even proclivity) for harm within cause or purposiveness can be found within all of us. The field of dark psychology assumes justifiably that these irrational desires to harm within us are incredibly complex and harm to understand.

Whether wrongdoing is purposive or even intentional, and whether it is done out of want of money, retaliation, or power, the most destructive force behind wrongdoing is aggression. Aggression is likely the single biggest adversary of prosocial relations, and it should not be confused with assertiveness. Aggression is any verbal and or physical behavior that is meant to harm or destroy. This aim is what differentiates it from other classes of behaviors that bring harm or destruction with no aims.

Biologically, there are certain genetic markers that are more indicative of aggression than others. Neurologically, it is the amygdala that controls most aggressive behavioral patterns. For this reason, people with enlarged and deformed amygdala typically commit violent acts at higher rates. As far as hormones are concerned, it is usually those people (primarily young men) with higher levels of testosterone and lower levels of serotonin who tend to be the most violent. The most aggressive people within societies are typically ones who have been put through something of a loop: their testosterone levels rise and cause them to become aggressive, which in turn begets higher levels of testosterone and even more aggression. In this way, some of the most dangerous people the world has to offer are created. Drugs and foods that increase serotonin and decrease testosterone levels are typically the best options for decreasing overall levels of aggression.

The most common cause of aggression is a failure or being stopped short of a goal. Studies indicate that those who have been made miserable by such unfortunate events usually make others around them more miserable as well. In these unpleasant instances, we naturally become frustrated, which begets our being angered, and once we are angered we can easily become aggressive if given a cue. Some of the most common stimuli that can cue aggressive behaviors are personal insults (perhaps the most common), cigarette smoke, foul odors, and hot temperatures. Ostracism is another common cause of aggression, causing some of the same neurological phenomena as physical pain does.

One of the most tragic causes of increased aggression is the knowledge that aggression can be rewarding in some instances. Children who learn early that aggression can pay out (so to speak) are much more likely to remain aggressive throughout life. Other social influences that can cause higher rates of aggression include the absence of one or both parents during the formative years, with the father figure usually being the one absent. In order to stop aggressive behavior before it starts, despite the family conditions, the best possible model to instill is one that rewards cooperation and sensitivity from an early age. Parents and caregivers should be models for these modes of conduct, but exasperated parents who do not have effective systems in place tend to become brash and even aggressive themselves with their children, often creating intergenerational lineages of aggression with their actions.

One of, if not the most, troubling aspects of human nature is sexual aggression. Rapes are typically committed by males against women. These have multifarious causes but are often of a mixture of sexual promiscuity (or the impersonal approach to sex) combined with hostile and aggressive masculinity.

In addition to the amygdala, the midbrain and the hypothalamus are also central in aggression, in all mammals. The hypothalamus has specialized receptors that determine levels of aggression based on the levels of serotonin and vasopressin that they are exposed to. Midbrain areas that deal with aggression have connections to both the brainstem and others structures such as the prefrontal cortex and the amygdala. Stimulation of the amygdala typically leads to higher levels of aggression within mammals, while lesions on this area (or on the hippocampus) typically lead to a reduction of the expression of social dominance out of the regulation of aggression and or fear.

The prefrontal cortex is an area crucial to the regulation of self-control and the inhibition of impulses, specifically aggressive ones. A reduction in the prefrontal cortex, particularly in its orbitofrontal and medial portions, is positively correlated with higher levels of violent and antisocial aggression. Response inhibition is also found to be lower in most violent offenders.

Again, a deficiency in serotonin levels is one of the most common causes of aggression and impulsivity. Lower levels of serotonin transmission can affect other neurochemical systems, including the dopamine system, which regulates motivation towards results and attention levels. Norepinephrine also influences levels of overall aggression, working within the hormonal system, the sympathetic nervous system, and the central nervous system. The neuropeptides oxytocin and vasopressin also play large roles in the regulation of social recognition, attachment, and aggression within mammals. Oxytocin plays its most important role in the regulation of female bonds with mates and offspring, as well as the use of protective and retaliatory aggression. Vasopressin is more so used for the regulation of aggression in males.

When we think of dark psychology one of the most common terms that comes to mind is "predator". Human predators come in all shapes and sizes and work to various means, but all of them have one thing in common if they are successful: persuasion. Predators of all types know who to "strum the strings that are inside all of us" as social psychologist Robert Cialdini puts it. These are people who look for attunement from all those who they come across, or the compliance to their own authority, whether it be real or imaginary.

The first thing that predators seek to establish over others is authority. They tend to look for the things that other people most desire, and then offer these things under the (usually false) guise of authority figures. They project confidence when around people who they think that they can influence. If they are well spoken then they usually are more successful in this practice, as we tend to question those who we find more well-spoken much less. One of the most fitting adjectives that could be used to describe most predators is impotence. These are typically people who have felt little to no power in their lives, being constantly subjected to the wills of others and never feeling that same sense of authority themselves, they start to seek our victims who they perceive as weaker than they are.

Another way in which predators operate to their ends is by fostering a sense of reciprocity within their victims. They will usually lure their victims in with gifts and or favors, only to trap them later with obligations to be fulfilled in order to pay back debts. These gifts and favors not only force victims to spend more time around their perpetrators but also divert their attention from the true aims of the predators. It is through this labyrinth of debts labors that victims can spend months to even years and decades of their lives in unnecessary contact with predatory people.

Similarity between people is one of the most common causes of liking. What more, once we have decided that we like another person we become much more likely to do things, things that they ask of us. This is why predators use many different ways to increase rapport with their victims, including the use of compliments, common identity, and common interests to trap their victims. In this way malevolent people can harm others without even being detected, only being perceived as friends and allies by their unwitting victims. Most predators are surprising to common people in that they are able to put on likable personas for themselves just as well as more benevolent people. They typically know how to imitate "normal" people with ease and seamlessness that allows them to work towards their malevolent ends without being detected by people with no expertise in the area of predation. Most are endowed with the same sense of conformity that we all are, but this conformity does not always apply to their actions as they manipulate their way through life.

Predators are always looking for what it is that potential victims want. Successful ones are able to easily tell what presses other people's buttons, and what it is that others most desire. Once they have ascertained what bait they should use to get what they want, they step in to provide the social proof to the victim that asserts that they are in the right and that they have everything that the victim is looking for. These are people who can almost smell our desires and insecurities, and who are ready and able to get the more gullible of us to do their bidding.

Since predators rely heavily on the power of commitment within their victims, they tend to seek out only people who they think will feel the most indebted to them. Initially, a predatory figure will elicit smaller commitments from their victims, which usually only lead into larger and larger ones as time goes on. When others let them, predators tend to pile on these commitments until it becomes difficult to disengage with them. This is usually when the darker side of the predator shows itself, and those who are in contact with him or her start to feel disillusioned.

If we want to avoid the predation of others, we have to introspect on our own vulnerabilities, as these are exactly the things that malevolent people are going to look for within us. We should also introspect on our own predatory behaviors as well, as none of us are immune to malevolence. Each one of us is both predatory and submissive, so reconciling these two selves is essential to better understanding ourselves and others.

# Chapter two: "Dark personality" traits

We tend to focus all too much on the lighter side of human psychology. Whether followers of the "positive psychology" movement or not, we often have difficulty seeing the value in the more rank underbelly of human psychology, the dark side. This happens to our detriment though, as it is the more bothersome aspects of our nature that tend to enlighten us more than the personas that people put on. Here we will delve into the darker traits of human psychology, the ones that all contain one overarching trait more destructive than any others: callousness or a lack of empathy for others. Those who have these traits are very diverse, but they all share the potential to harm others due to their inability to empathize.

The first of these traits, and perhaps the most common is narcissism. We all display this negative trait at one point or another, so it is usually best to reserve judgment when others come across as narcissistic upon first glance. Narcissists often disregard the thoughts and feelings of others and take advantage of people in order to get what they want. Witnessing other people getting attention and admiration frustrates them, as they believe that they are entitled to these things above others. This trait, like any other, exists on a spectrum within people, with the most pretentious of us at the top and the ones with least self-efficacy at the bottom.

Although all of us experience narcissistic traits in varying degrees, in around 1% of the population these traits can take on a more severe, pathological form in which the person gains an unrealistic perception of his or her own abilities and is in constant need of attention and admiration. This pathologized form of narcissism is called narcissistic personality disorder.

Narcissistic supply is a sort of admiration, sustenance, or interpersonal support drawn by a narcissist out of his or her environment. This supply can easily become essential to the maintenance of the narcissist's self-esteem if it is never kept from him or her. For this reason, narcissists tend to seek out those who will admire them irrationally and there is very little that will stop a narcissist once he or she has found some sort of relationship in which there are unjustified resources allocated interpersonally. This need for the admiration or attention of codependents is considered pathological because it does not take into account the feeling, thoughts, and or needs of the other people involved. The narcissist only considers his or her supply and is never focused on what is actually going on with those other people involved.

Narcissistic injury is a perceived threat to the narcissist's self-esteem. Other terms interchangeable with this one are narcissistic blow, narcissistic scar, and narcissistic wound. What all of these have in common, however, is what they are met with narcissistic rage. Narcissistic rage is a common reaction to any form of narcissistic injury. This rage (like any other sort of rage) exists within a continuum, ranging from mild remoteness to harsher expressions of annoyance and frustration, and finally to intense emotional outbursts, sometimes including violent attacks.

Narcissistic rage can manifest itself in many other ways as well. These include depressive, paranoid delusion, and catatonic episodes. It is also widely held that most narcissists have two main types of rage. The first of these types is rage constantly directed at one or more other people, while the second type is constantly directed at the self. Narcissistic rage is not necessarily troublesome in its severity, as its severity exists on a similar spectrum as does "normal" rage, but becomes more problematic when considering that it is inherently pathological.

A narcissistic defense is any process whereby the idealized self portrait of the narcissist is preserved, while any of its actual limitations are denied. In other words, this type of defense is found when the narcissist is trying to preserve his or her own self image more so than trying to ascertain the truth about the self. These defenses tend to be very rigid, as the narcissist anchors as much as possible to the most self flattering narratives imaginable. Most narcissists actually do experience feelings of guilt or shame (both conscious and unconscious) quite often, and one of the most common methods by which they alleviate these negative feelings is by putting up such defenses. Pathological narcissism has to find psychological shortcuts in order to survive throughout greater self-realization, and narcissistic defense is likely the most common of these shortcuts.

The original definition of narcissistic abuse referred more to the abuse committed by narcissistic parents on their children. Typically, this type of abuse consists of the children of narcissists having to give up parts of their own feelings and wants in order to protect their parents' self-esteems. Children who grow up being subjected to this type of abuse often have codependency issues later on in life. Having no knowledge of what constitutes a normal relationship, they tend to be unable to recognize who it is who they will be better off with and who to avoid. It is common that they will formulate further relationships with more narcissists who have similar pathologies to those of their parents.

In more recent years this term has been more widely applied to abuse within relationships among adults. Adult narcissists are about as likely to abuse other adults as they are to abuse children. These abusive relationships typically do not last as long due to the fact that adult victims usually have much more mobility to get out of the relationships than do child victims.

The next dark trait is Machiavellianism. This term can be applied to both the political philosophy of Niccolò Machiavelli and a manipulative personality trait. Here only the later usage will apply. This trait is most commonly characterized by a deceitful personality style, a pathological focus on personal gain and self-interest, an overall deficiency of empathy, and a blatant disregard for morality.

One of the most troubling aspects of Machiavellians is their overall lack of emotion. This often leads them to be influenced very little by "conventional" modes of morality and to subsequently manipulate and deceive others without remorse in order to meet their own personal needs. This trait is measured in units called machs by psychologists. People with higher levels of machs are shown to agree more with statements such as "never tell others your reasoning unless it benefits you to do so", and less with statements such as "people are generally good", "there is never an excuse to lie to others", or "the most successful among us lead moral lives". Typically, males score higher levels of machs than do females.

Machiavellians are typically rather cold and selfish people who see others mostly as instruments they can use to serve their own interests. The motives that they have in mind at any given point in time, whether they be sexual, social, professional, etc., are often pursued in duplicitous manners, with little to no thought of the wellbeing of the other parties involved in mind. Those with higher levels of machs tend to be motivated more by power, money, and competition than anything else, while those with lower levels of machs tend to focus more on things such as family commitment, self-love, and community building. People with higher levels of machs want to win at any cost, no matter how steep. With these views in mind, we could reasonably argue that people who are more Machiavellian than others are also more bent toward avarice. These people are typically much less motivated by altruistic sentiments and any forms of philanthropy, and instead, spend most of their time in aimless competition and malevolent industry. For these reasons, Machiavellians are usually much less trustworthy and much more self-interested than others.

It is only their outstanding abilities in manipulating others that give Machiavellians the reputation of being an intelligent group of people. In reality, there is no verifiable correlation between machs and IQ scores, but the stereotype of the intelligent Machiavellian shifting his or her way through vast webs of action and coming out with everything in mind persists, nevertheless. Emotional intelligence is, however, not a strong point of most Machiavellians. Higher levels of machs are typically correlated with lower EQ scores. Both emotional recognition and emotional empathy are negatively correlated with Machiavellianism. This trait has also never been shown to be correlated to a more advanced theory of mind. This suggests that Machiavellians are not necessarily better able to understand what others are thinking in social situations, so any abilities in manipulation they might possess are not related to their theory of mind.

Among some psychological circles, Machiavellianism is considered to be merely a subclinical form of psychopathy. While this personality trait is closely related to psychopathy and overlaps with it in several areas of thought, most psychologists hold that it is, in fact, an entirely independent personality construct. Psychopaths are generally much more impulsive and have less self-control than Machiavellians. Both of these traits do share dishonesty, however. Machiavellians are also typically much less agreeable and conscientious than the general population, which often leads to their finding little success in their careers and personal relationships. Machiavellians are also high in agency and low in communion, meaning that they seek to individuate and succeed more than they seek work with others in communal efforts. This is not necessarily a bad combination of traits in of itself, but what is troubling about many Machiavellians is that they often desire not only to succeed themselves but also seek actively to do so at the expense of others.

What makes many Machiavellians so effective in what they do is their ability to stay under people's radars. There are, however, some fundamental ways in which we can clearly identify these dangerous people before they start to wreak havoc on our lives.

One of the greatest indicators of truly high machs in a person is that person's ability to function especially well in workplaces and other social situations in which the rules are ambiguous. With no clear cut boundaries, these people are going to inevitably roam in every direction they see fit, and will constantly be thinking of ways to advance their own interests at the costs of the company that they keep. Machiavellians thrive most where lines are blurred and all behaviors seem unprecedented, because where these vulnerable settings exist they see opportunities to take actions that they will not be held responsible for.

Another red flag is excessive emotional detachment, sometimes coupled with a cynical outlook on things that enables the person to wait patiently and passionlessly for any opportunities that might present themselves. With this impulse control, Machiavellians are better able to plan ahead and to determine what they can do to manipulate than others are.

Machiavellians are also characterized by their use of pressure, guilt, self-disclosure, charm, and politeness in order to meet their ends. These tactics allow them to maneuver socially toward their malevolent goals without being detected. In addition to using these tactics, they also prepare backup plans to cut themselves out of corners when they are caught. Endless excuses and diversions are often employed when they are outed, the multiplicity of which can be overwhelming to those who do try to expose them.

The true potency of Machiavellianism lies within its covertness. These people are able to manipulate others so effectively because, in part, no one suspects them of harboring ulterior motives in the things that they do. Under the guise of normal, benevolent people they are often able to blend seamlessly into the foliage of wholesome citizenry.

Psychopathy is perhaps the most well-known and disturbing of the dark traits. Psychopathy as a personality disorder is characterized by ongoing antisocial behaviors, impaired capacity to empathize, and certain egotistical, disinhibited, and bold traits.

There are two mains types of psychopathy, characterized by their symptoms. The first (and less problematic) type is known as Cleckleyan psychopathy, characterized by disinhibited and bold behavioral patterns. The second type is criminal psychopathy, characterized by more aggressive and disinhibited behaviors, in this case, criminal. Of these two types, the latter is obviously more paid attention to due to the fact that a large portion of the world's most notorious criminals have suffered from this type of psychopathy.

The first of the psychopathic traits is often the one that allows all others to become unmanageable: boldness. This trait is constituted by a low level of fear combined with a high stress tolerance, a general toleration of danger and uncertainty, and incredibly high levels of assertiveness and self-confidence. An excess of this trait may or may not be related to individual variations of the amygdala, the brain's most important regulator of fear. With this boldness psychopaths are often able to handle people and situations that normal people would much rather shy away from. This can work the advantage of the psychopath but does often get him or her into more trouble than is necessary. With this trait, psychopaths often have a hard time distinguishing actual threats from normal occurrences, because their neural circuitry is simply not indicating to them that things are one way or the other.

Disinhibition is the next trait of psychopaths. This term refers to a lack of impulse control combined with issues concerning planning, a lack of control over urges, a constant need to instant gratification, and an overall poor restraints on behavior. This trait in excess often corresponds with impairments in structures within the frontal lobe that influences these types of behavioral control systems.

Disinhibition causes many psychopaths to act impulsively and even erratically when following their immediate desires. Always living for the moment, they never have a clear sight of what might happen next or what they should do to give themselves lasting gratification. This often leads them to make worse decisions which damage them more because so many of the things that give us instant gratification end up harming us greatly in the long run.

Another common trait of psychopaths is that of meanness or cruelty. Psychopaths often lack empathy and have little to no intimate relationships with others, sometimes even being disdainful of the company of others. They often use cruelty in order to obtain greater power, are generally much more exploitative than others, recalcitrant towards authority figures, and tend to seek out excitement in careless and dangerous fashions. This trait is likely more destructive to those who come into contact with psychopaths than any of the others mentioned here. Psychopaths typically do not enjoy the company of others, so when they are around others they are all the more likely to act in cruel and callous manners because they perceive that they have nothing to lose. This outlook on others causes them to act in ways that are disagreeable and sometimes dangerous, whether with a purposiveness for doing so in mind or not.

Typically, psychopaths are rather high in antagonism, and very low in conscientiousness and in anxiety, feeling almost no anxiety, in fact. These people are also low in socialization and responsibility and high in sensation seeking, impulsivity, and aggression. The combination of these traits tend to create people who do not get along with others well, who contribute little product to society at large, and who follow their impulses freely and without anxiety.

Of the other dark personality traits, psychopathy is probably most closely related to narcissism. One psychological perspective, in fact, even considers this trait as just another part of the pathological narcissism spectrum. Some psychologists assert that narcissistic personality exists on the bottom of this spectrum, malignant narcissism in the middle, and psychopathy at its highest point.

Socially, the main symptoms of psychopathy are callousness, manipulation, and sometimes crime and violence. Mentally, the impairment of processes related to cognition and affect are the biggest indicators of psychopathy. These symptoms usually start to come about around adolescence, though they are sometimes found even in younger children and are at other times not found until later in adulthood.

Psychopathy scores are surprisingly telltale concerning incarceration records. Higher scores of this trait are often found to be correlated with a repeated bout of imprisonment, holdings within higher security areas of detention centers, more disciplinary infractions, and higher rates of substance abuse.

While psychopathy is not entirely synonymous with violence, there are lots of well noted correlations between this trait and violent acts. Psychopathy is often characterized by "instrumental" aggression. This form of aggression is more proactive and or predatory than others are. Subdued emotion and goals not directed but largely facilitated by the causing of harm are two other characteristics of this potent form of aggression. Instrumental aggression is often correlated with homicide offenses because of the predatory nature of this form of aggression.

Psychopathy is also linked to domestic violence, with around 15-30% of perpetrators showing psychopathic tendencies. It is mainly the callousness, combined with the disdain of interpersonal connections, that causes many psychopaths to commit domestic violence offences. Despite all of these connections that psychopathy has with various types of violent criminal behavior, psychopathic tendencies are still not widely considered in risk assessment.

Sex crime is another gruesome sort of criminal activity that is commonly associated with psychopathy due to a psychopathic proclivity towards violent sexual behavior. The relationship between psychopathy and child molestation is shown in the number of offences by the perpetrator, which tends to rise in more psychopathic individuals. Tendencies towards sadistic violence and a lack or remorse tend to cause psychopaths to commit sex crimes that normal people would simply never imagine. Despite this disconcerting proclivity to reoffend, psychopaths are on average 2.5 times more likely to be granted conditional releases than are their non-psychopathic counterparts when imprisoned for their crimes.

Psychopathy is also correlated with organized crime, war crime, and economic crime. It is the antisocial violence, the worldview that precludes the welfare of others, the incessant externalization of blame, the lack of remorse, and the impulsivity that tends to drive psychopaths towards criminal behaviors of all kinds at higher rates than non-psychopaths. While terrorism is popularly associated with psychopathy, psychopaths are actually less likely to engage in terrorist activity because of the planning, organization, and frequent communal working that goes into staging terrorist attacks. Terrorism appeals less to psychopaths because of their own selfish intuitions as well.

In childhood and adolescence, the most common precursors of psychopathy are emotionlessness or callousness, impulsivity or responsibility, and narcissism. The trait and or personality disorder can be so difficult to discern or to diagnose within these early stages because its symptoms are found in so many non-psychopathic children and adolescents. These traits are, whether found in psychopaths or normal individuals, often indicative of later violent or criminal behavior. In juveniles, psychopathy is usually correlated with higher rates of negative emotions such as depression, anxiety, hostility, and anger. Although we may have certain indicators of psychopathy in younger people, these indicators usually to not manifest themselves into actual psychopathy later on in life and are typically individual issues instead.

Conduct disorder in juveniles is seen as a pathway to later antisocial personality disorder and psychopathy. This disorder usually stems from a toxic mixture of preexisting neurological issues and prolonged exposure to adverse environmental factors. Not only do those with this disorder display prolonged antisocial behaviors throughout life, but they are also shown to remain in poorer overall health and usually have much lower socio economic status. Childhood onset starts before 10 and typically results in more long term antisocial behavior, while adolescent onset starts after 10 and more often results in antisocial behavior limited to the short term.

It is when conduct disorder is intermixed with ADHD that the antisocial behaviors associated with it become their most problematic. Younger people with this combination of disorders tend to show the same callousness, aggression, and behavioral inhibition as psychopaths of all ages display. The remorseless and unemotional interpersonal style of those with conduct disorder is one of psychology's most remarkable parallels to psychopathy.

As far as mentality is concerned, dysfunctions within the amygdala and the prefrontal cortex are the most common neurological causes of psychopathy. These dysfunctions are often inborn, though they are at other times caused by tumors, legions, and traumatic brain injuries sustained by these regions. While patients with these issues in these regions may resemble in thought and action psychopaths, they are divorced from the latter group. Whether psychopathic or non-psychopathic, people with damage to the regions of the brain typically have a much more difficult time learning social and moral reasoning than most people do. Stimulus reinforced learning is also impaired within individuals with damage to these regions, meaning that whether being rewarded or punished, these people have difficulty learning based on what effects are stemming from what they are doing.

Despite these learning defects, there is no unassailable link between psychopathy and IQ. Regarding intelligence, psychopaths as a group are really a rather accurate reflection of the general population, with some being incredibly brilliant and some being very dull by contrast, while the majority is about average.

Psychopathy is also linked to unusual responses to distress cues. Vocal and physical responses to fear and sadness are often either looked over or misinterpreted by psychopaths usually because of a decrease in activity within the fusicore and extrastriate regions of the brain. This inactivity results in the failure to recognize all emotions on other people's faces as well, but it is the inability to discern fear and sadness that usually works most to the detriment of psychopaths.

Amorality is one of the more problematic byproducts of psychopathy. Here this term refers to a disregard for, an indifference towards, or just an absence of moral sentiments and practices. There are two main areas of concern within most moral reasoning: personal transgressions and compliance (or noncompliance) with conventional rules. Socrates noted these areas as the adherence of natural and conventional laws respectively. When asked to determine which types of these laws should be followed more closely, psychopaths generally assert that it is the conventional laws whereas non-psychopaths usually believe that natural or personal laws should be adhered to first. This tendency could suggest that psychopaths do not have strong moral laws laid out for themselves and are more inclined to only follow those of the systems in which they find themselves.

While there is no notable preference among psychopaths between the infliction of personal and interpersonal harm, these people are usually much less averse to inflicting interpersonal harm than are non-psychopaths. Those psychopaths with the lowest levels of anxiety are usually much more likely to inflict personal harm.

There are moderate genetic links or causes of psychopathy, but these are not quite as substantial as the environmental ones. The most common environmental causes of psychopathy all stem from early experiences in childhood and adolescence, including but not limited to coming from a disrupted family with a young or depressed mother, low involvement of the father, having convicted parents, physical neglect, low family income or social status, poor housing and or supervision, large family size, harsh discipline, and delinquent sibling(s).

Head injuries are also strongly linked with violence and psychopathy. It is the injuries to the prefrontal and orbitofrontal cortices that do the most harm to suffers, with impairments in social and moral reasoning being the most disconcerting effects of these injuries. Damage to the ventromedial cortex is also concerning, usually causing a reduction in autonomic responses, inability to make evasive maneuvers, impaired economic decision making, and diminished expressions of guilt, shame, and empathy.

Psychopathy is likely the most famous of the dark traits due to the destructiveness of its sufferers. Many of the world's most notorious criminals have been or are psychopathic, but this does not entail that all psychopaths are criminals. Some of them, in fact, go on to lead normal, productive lives in which they contribute greatly to society as a whole.

Now we come to sadism. Sadomasochism (or SM, as we will call it here) is the receiving of giving of pleasure stemming from the infliction of pain and or humiliation. Often sadists receive sexual gratification from the infliction of this pain, whether they are the ones giving it or the ones receiving it. These practices are, surprisingly, usually consensual, and so differ from non-consensual sex crimes.

The origin of the term sadism is found in Marquis De Sade (1740-1814), who both practiced sadistic sex rituals and wrote about them. The term masochism comes from Leopold Von Sacher-Masoch, who wrote novels about his own masochistic sex practices.

Some psychologists consider pain and violence to be at the center of the sadomasochistic practice, while others look more towards dominance and submission. In reality, most sadomasochists are interested in both. Sigmund Freud considered the first "form" of sadomasochism to be centered around the notion of cuckoldry (or the choosing of rivals as mates), and the second form to not concern itself with relationships at all and to be interested instead on the pageantry of the sexual practices.

Each sadomasochist finds the practices associated with the disorder appealing to his or her own reasons. Often, the SMs who prefer to take on more submissive roles within their practices do so out of a need to escape from the guilt, responsibility, and stress of life. Being in the presence of strong and domineering figures instills a sense of safety and security for others. Sadists, on the other hand, may enjoy taking on more domineering roles out of a desire to feel more empowered. Whether sadistic or masochistic, SMs are simply trying to fulfill emotional needs that they have, which often stem from childhood experiences and relationships. While these needs are met in ways some would find unusual or inappropriate, as long as these practices are consensual we will usually be wise to avoid judgment.

Finally, sociopathy (or antisocial personality disorder) is a personality disorder marked by a lack of remorse or guilt regarding wrongdoing inflicted onto others. This disorder is so similar to psychopathy that many psychologists in the past have considered it a sub disorder within a larger class of psychopathic disorders, but most today hold that sociopathy is a separate disorder all together. The same manipulation tactics, impulsivity, lack of guilt, and excess of aggression found in psychopaths and Machiavellians are shared by sociopaths.

While some sociopaths are high functioning and contribute great things to society, most have difficulties remaining responsible throughout life due to their impulsivity and often lead shorter lifespans than average as a result of reckless practices such as substance abuse and criminal activity.

While there is a noted genetic component to the development of antisocial personality disorder, there remains also certain environmental factors that can put young people at a greater risk of developing this disorder. These include but are not limited to never being taught to respect the rights of others, poor discipline, the presence of negative role models, and alcoholism as well as other forms of substance abuse, both in parents and in their children.

Conduct disorder and ADHD before the age of 10 is yet another indicator of later development of antisocial personality disorder. Some studies have even indicated that 25% of girls and 40% of boys who develop conduct disorder throughout development go on to develop antisocial personality disorder later on in adulthood.

The most common symptoms of sociopathy are as follows: the repeated committing of unlawful acts, lying or manipulating in order to achieve results, impulsivity, repeated fighting or assaults, disregard for the safety of the self and of others, a lack of empathy and remorse, and personal and financial irresponsibility. In order to be formally diagnosed with sociopathy, a person must exhibit at least three of the symptoms listed above. Other criteria that need to be met in order to diagnose one with antisocial personality disorder are that the person is at least 18 years old and that he or she has been diagnosed as having conduct disorder onset before or at the age of 15. Typically, there is some time of antisocial episode and a subsequent intervention taken place before a person is officially diagnosed with this disorder as most do not suspect of or admit to themselves having sociopathy. These episodes are not, however, necessary for a formal diagnosis of this troublesome disorder.

These symptoms usually peak when the sufferer is in his or her early twenties. Once he or she has reached the 40s, however, some find that these symptoms curtail and eliminate themselves.

Talk therapy is the most common and effective form of therapy for this disorder and is usually the same for all of the other dark personality traits. This form of therapy is helpful for these people because, in part, it offers a way for the individual to develop his or her interpersonal skills. The first goal within these therapies is, however, always the reduction of impulsive behaviors which may lead to criminal harm done.

There are surprisingly very little medications that help mitigate the symptoms of antisocial personality disorder. In addition, to talk therapy, clinicians also give schema therapies to many patents, which aim to edit and better organize maladaptive patterns of thought often stemming from childhood. The writer here would argue that this form of therapy should be more widely used among all those who suffer from dark personality traits, regardless of what those traits might be, though this is merely opinion.

# Chapter three: Studies of dark psychology

There are no better assertions of dark psychological happenings than the actual studies conducted on the topic. We should now go over some of the most famous examples of such studies, pouring over both their reasons for having taken place and their significance after the fact.

The Asch experiments of the 1950s were conducted to ascertain to what degree an individual's opinions can be influenced by those of the majority of the group the individual finds him or herself in. Solomon Asch, the leader of these experiments, started these out by having young male college students participate in perceptual tasks. He divided the participants into groups, with all but one of the members in each group being "confederates" or actors. The goal of these experiments was to analyze how the one "genuine" participant would react to the thoughts and actions of all of the actors.

With all other participants having pre-scripted responses to all questions asked, the responses of the one genuine participant became the only true independent variables in the study. With varying degrees of peer pressure applied to the one real participant, the effects of this pressure were then seen and studied in their various degrees of severity.

Each participant was simply asked a series of questions, such as which line was the shortest or longer within a series. Initially, all of the "confederates" gave correct answers to all of the questions asked in order to avoid making the one genuine participant suspicious. It was only later on that some incorrect answers started to be added.

There was a control group among the normal groups when these experiments were taking place, in which no peer pressure was applied to participants. Within this control group, only around one out of every 35 answers were incorrect, a statistic likely attributable to mere experimental error. Within the normal groups, on the others hand, one third of the genuine participants gave an incorrect answer when others within the group had also done so. This implies that people are in fact much more likely to make incorrect judgments when the majority of those around them are doing the same.

At least ¾ of all participants gave at least one incorrect answer to the questions given to them. Within this experiment, people hid their own opinions, whether they were genuinely suspicious of their own intuitions, or were simply wanting to comply more with their company.

While we all tend to pride ourselves on being independently minded and fully autonomous individuals, studies like this one indicate that at times we behave like anything but. This issue of conformity vs. individuality is an age old struggle which some of the greatest minds in history have poured over tirelessly. Typically, moderation should be kept about when determining the relationship between our own opinions and those of the group(s) we find ourselves in. To trust our own intuitions entirely and without question would be arrogant, and could potentially plunge us into ignorance of the reality of our own making, one which could have easily been avoided by receptiveness to the opinions of others. We should also keep in mind that other people are just as susceptible to error as we are, and that might do not always make right. In following the pack blindly we are subjecting ourselves to whatever this pack may have in mind for us. Just because more people believe in something does not make that something more or less true. Bandwagons are great in that they make us feel like we are a part of something, but potentially destructive when we put too much faith in them.

It is not an example of personal darkness to deviate from the well-trodden paths of our company. While larger groups may provide order for their constituents, this order can easily become tyranny if not checked. When no one is around to verify the validity of any of the views of the group, the whole system tends to collapse in on itself, leaving the most dogmatic at the very bottom of the rubble. History gives us countless examples of people doing horrible things out of subservience to their tribe(s).

The Asch experiments are merely a microcosmic reflection of this destructive tendency.

The bible tells one story of the good Samaritan, who stops to help a man in need while other, self-righteous people simply pass on by. John Darley and C. Daniel Batson, inspired by this famous story, wanted to see if there was any correlation between religiosity and helpfulness, and so conducted the good Samaritan experiment.

Three main hypotheses were on the researchers minds when heading into this experiment: that people thinking helpful religious thoughts would ultimately be no more inclined to help others than anyone else, that people who were in a rush would be less likely to help others, and that those who are religious simply for gain will be much less likely to help others than will people who are religious out of a want to find meaning in life. People of a Samaritan fashion will be more likely to help than people of a Levite fashion.

After recruiting seminary students for this experiment, the research conducted a questionnaire on religion on the participants in order to later ascertain the accuracy of the third hypothesis. They then started the experiment in one building, only to ask the participants to walk over to another building to finish the experiment. On the way there the participants found a man slumped over in an alleyway and had no knowledge of what was wrong with him or why he was there.

Before having the participants depart, they told different groups different pieces of information regarding urgency and what they would have to do in the other buildings. One of the tasks was related to seminary jobs and the other was related to the telling of the story of the good Samaritan. One of these groups was told that it was late and needed to head over to the other building right away, while the other group was told that it had a few minutes.

The man in the alleyway was cued to moan and cough twice while the participants passed by. The researchers set up a scale of helping beforehand which was organized as follows: 0= failure to notice the victim and his need, 1= noticing the need but offering no aid, 2= made no stop but did decide to help indirectly (telling their aide upon arrival), 3= stopping and asking the victim if he needed help, 4= stopping and helping the victim, leaving him aside afterwards, 5= refusing to leave the victim after stopping and offering help, or insistence on taking him somewhere else.

After the subjects arrived at the second location they had them answer a second questionnaire, this one regarding helpfulness. The sense of urgency had an effect on the helping of the man in the alleyway. All in all, around 40% of the participants chose to help the victim. Those who were not very rushed helped

63% of the time, those who were somewhat rushed helped 40% of the time, and those who were very rushed helped only 10% of the time. The Sammarinese here helped 53% of the time, while the Levites only helped 29% of the time, thereby confirming the third hypothesis. This study could ultimately find no correlation between religiosity and helpful behavior. Those who were more interested in helpfulness as a good in itself tended to be much more helpful than those who saw religion as a means of getting things that they wanted.

Even when on the way to give a speech about the good Samaritan, a person in a hurry is much less likely to help others around him or her. This just goes to show that thinking about ethics does not necessarily cause us to act more ethically. The relationship between urgency and helpfulness should also be taken note of, as this could indicate that as our lives are becoming more and more fast paced with each passing year we are bound to become less and less ethical, though this is just one take that could be had on this phenomena. There is one other possible explanation to the lack of help: the conflict between the needs of the experimenter vs. those of the victim could have affected the participants' decision making more so than any callousness on their part.

This experiment remains controversial in that it takes on religion, but only the unreasonable would deny that religion is better used by those who simply seek meaning in life than by those who are driven merely by avarice. There is simply no room for morality were people are desirous of more things. When we are overwhelmed by the multifarious wants that we have, we always open up pandora's box in order to meet them, letting all of the evilest things that we can imagine roam the earth simply out of greed. Charity really is a good in of itself. From a utilitarian standpoint, it is almost always better to be more charitable because the happiness derived from doing so is not only felt in our beneficiaries but in ourselves as well.

This study also shows us that in order to promote the good and avoid the bad we are going to have to take time out of our days to do so. Haste in our actions makes us much less likely to help others. When we are constantly busy with our own activities we sometimes fail to recognize the needs of others, but stopping to do so every once in a while will benefit us greatly in the long run.

The bystander apathy experiment of 1968 conducted by John Darley and Bibb Latane sought to explore one of the most interesting, and perhaps disappointing, phenomena in the field of social psychology. Within this type of experiment, an emergency is staged with one participant among several other confederates. These researchers would then study how long it took the participant to act if he or she chose to do so at all. Surprisingly, this study showed us all that we are much less likely to help others when in the company of a crowd. Around 70% of participants helped when no others were involved, while only 40% chose to do so in the company of groups.

This reluctance to help others when in crowds may stem from mere self-consciousness, or it could also be due to a perception that being the one who helps first is to take on something of a leadership role, a role which most people are averse to taking up for themselves. For whatever reason it may occur, this tendency to neglect those in need is problematic for obvious reasons. No matter what the trouble happens to be, we are more likely to avoid it when we find ourselves in larger groups, as this experiment would seem to suggest.

The Stanford prison experiment, perhaps the most well-known of any mentioned here, was conducted in 1971 by Philip Zimbardo with an aim to study what psychological effects are entailed in becoming either a prisoner or a prison guard. Here 24 male subjects were taken and randomly selected to be either guards or prisoners within a mock prison in the basement of the Stanford psychology building.

Zimbardo was reportedly impressed at how quickly the subjects adapted to their roles, as the guards quickly took on more and more authoritarian roles and eventually even resorted to the psychological torture of the prisoners. Not only did the prisoners take the psychological abuse passively, they even went so far as to harass other prisoners at the requests of the guards. It was not until after Zimbardo himself started to condone the abuse that two prisoners quit the experiment early and it was all stopped after only six days.

Impressionability and obedience tend to rise greatly when people have access to an ideology that makes them feel legitimized and institutional and social support, as this study would suggest. This study also goes to show the effects of cognitive dissonance and the power of authority. When we are under the control of a system that we perceive as having a strong, centralized basis of power, we tend to become very willing to follow the wants of that system, whatever they might be. We also become highly impressed upon by that system. When conflicts of interests between ourselves and the will of the system arise, cognitive dissonance follows, which is resolved by more obedience in most people. This study also demonstrates our tendency to let authority figures get away with doing whatever they have in mind.

This study is considered situational rather than dispositional behaviors, meaning that the behaviors noted here we more a result of the situation at hand than one of the personalities of the participants. Whether the guards had a disposition towards committing abuse, or whether the prisoners were disposed towards passivity is not a matter of concern here. The only thing studied here is the situational behavior of those involved.

This study tells us so much about prison life. To reflect on what would have happened had the guards never been stopped does raise some other questions though. It is not clear what would have ever checked the power of Zimbardo in this study. He had the power to essentially do anything to the subjects, so this study can also be analyzed as an inquiry into the issue of unchecked power.

The Milgram experiments of 1961, conducted by Stanley Milgram, is one of the most insightful studies of authority in the field of social psychology. Here the objective was to record the willingness of participants to perform tasks that went against their own personal consciousness when these tasks had been assigned by an authority figure.

Milgram conducted these experiments with the trials of Nazi war criminals in mind, asking himself one central question: did all of these war criminals have a shared sense of morality? These studies, on the whole, confirmed that people often perform actions that go against their strongest moral beliefs when compelled to by authority figures. While these studies proved to be scientifically valid and useful, many considered and still consider them to have been unethical, entailing both physical and psychological abuse that scared the participants for life.

Milgram recruited 40 men to take part in these experiments. These was a shock generator used, the shocks of which started at 30 volts and increased by 15 volt increments until finally reaching 450, many of them owning such labels as "slight shock", "moderate shock", and "danger: severe shock". The final two switched on this generator were simply labeled "xxx".

These participants of this experiment took on the role of the "teacher", who would administer shocks when the confederates would give incorrect answers given to them. Although these shocks were not really administered, the teachers believed them to be and the confederates would act as though they had been shocked when they were administered.

As the voltage would continually increase as the experiment went on, the student would ask to be released and some would even complain of heart conditions. Once the 300 volt threshold had been crossed over, the student would start to bang on the walls of the room and would thereafter refuse to answer any further questions. This silence, as the teachers were instructed, was supposed to be taken as an incorrect answer, so more shocks were administered when the questions were not answered.

Most of the students asked the teachers whether or not they should continue, to which they were given the standard replies: "please continue", "the experiment requires that you continue", "it is absolutely essential that you continue", and "you have no other choice, you must continue".

The level of shock that each participant was willing to deliver was the indicator of their obedience. It was initially predicted that only around 3 out of every 100 participants would agree to administer the maximum shocks. In reality, an astonishing 65% of them would actually go on to administer these shocks, and each participant involved would administer the 300 volt shocks. This shows that people are even more compliant than most expect them to be and that we can easily be compelled to actions that we find objectionable when under the influence of authority figures.

The Milgram experiment shows us that we are, in many cases, willing to go so far as to kill others if instructed to do so by an authority figure who we deem to have moral and or legal authority. This obedience is learned early on in life within us and is adapted and reinforced in many different ways throughout the courses of our lives. We all know that we naturally tend to go with wishes of those who have more power than us, but the Milgram experiments teach us just to what extend this tendency carries through within our actions.

According to Milgram, we fall into one of two states behaviorally within social situations: the autonomous state (in which people direct their own actions) and the agentic state (in which people let others direct their actions). Milgram asserts that we need the following criteria to be met for us to enter into the agentic state of behavior: the person giving orders is perceived as being qualified, and that the order taker trusts the ordered to take responsibility for anything that goes wrong.

Agency theory suggests that it is only when we feel responsible for our own actions that we truly start to act with autonomy. While putting responsibility into the hands of others may be relieving, we have to be responsible for what we are doing if we are to remain autonomous actors.

The studies here mentioned, among many others, show the darker underbelly of the human psyche. While it may be hard to accept that we are flawed in the ways that these studies prove us to be, doing so will always lead us to better and more honest lives, fully aware of our both our unassailable successes and catastrophic failures.

# Chapter four: Mind reading

Mind reading is mainly a game of three factors: sensory information, in-person body cues, and social cues. Without attention paid to these three aspects of communication any attempt at delving into the thoughts and feelings of others becomes fruitless. Today we typically communicate more so through text messages, IMs, emails, and phone calls than through real interpersonal conversations. This entails that we tend to miss out on learning the finer points of real communications, and are subsequently far less able to tell what others are thinking. Screen time seems to be the most destructive thing for us in the way of telling what others are thinking.

For better or worse, we can usually tell what others are thinking with or without the aid of what they are actually saying. The words are often just the tip of the iceberg when it comes to what is actually going on within other people's minds. When most hear the term "mind reading" they tend to think of psychics, witches, and other people of this sort, but great steps can be taken by anyone to better understand the thoughts of others. With just a little guidance and a lot of practice, anyone can become just as proficient in the art of telling what others are thinking as the more mystical figures among us.

So much of interpersonal human connection is dependent upon our ability to guess at and respond to the thoughts and actions of others appropriately that we often have difficulty reconciling what is actually being said by others with what impressions we are getting from them. In order to understand the thoughts of others, we must first delve into our own. It is all too easy for an attempt at understanding what another person is thinking to quickly turn into a judgment. We jump to conclusions about the people we meet and often run into errors as a result.

One of the greatest obstacles we face we trying to mind read is that of dishonesty or a lack of expression in the words or the nonverbal cues of those who we are talking to. When we come across people with good poker faces and or dishonest people, our tendency gauge language and nonverbal cues are of little use to us. There are, however, many ways in which we can dig beneath the superficial aspects of the communication and get a glimpse at what it really going on within our partner's minds.

In order to read minds, we must first trust our own intuition. This involves developing a more trustworthy intuition though, which is a task that is always becoming and never being. Here we should avoid some of the magical thinking that often goes into the habit of mind reading and only use our reason. A willingness to look into the places that we least want to and to challenge our own beliefs is also crucial here because if we go into trying to read the minds of others already anchored to our own beliefs our findings will always be less fruitful. For example, if I am convinced of the pretentiousness of a person right at meeting them and never think to challenge this conviction, I will never be granted greater insight into their character because I have already categorized them. We do not need to have esoteric powers in order to mind read, we only need to be open and reasonable when communicating with others.

Mindfulness is one of the greatest skills that we can home in on in order to read minds more effectively. This practice allows us to clear our minds of any needless distractions and worries, enabling us to pay greater attention to those who we are speaking with. When we have our heads fully grated on our own inner worries and problems we can never delve into what is going on with others fully. Any ability that we may have had in the way of understanding other people's thoughts falls by the wayside as we try to pick up our own pieces with cluttered and anxiety riddled psyches. Here it becomes clear that if we want to determine what is going on within other people's inner lives we are first going to have to look at our own. Doing so will give us the clarity and the energy necessary for reading the minds of others.

The first step towards better reading the minds of others is always to maintain an open spirit for doing so. Without this openness, we will never reap the full rewards of what other people are communicating to us. This openness does necessarily have to come with a certain degree of intolerance though, intolerance directed at anything that does not immediately serve whatever purposes we have in the present moment. When we try to take in all things, including those things that have nothing to do with us, we always get overwhelmed and feel as though we are making no progress toward our goals, because we probably are not. When we instead remain open only to the things that are affecting us directly we usually find that we have much more energy to understand others and to work with what we have accordingly.

Again, mindfulness training of some kind is the best practice we have to foster this sense of openness. Stress and distraction cause us to not only extract less information out of others but to also misinterpret what little that we do get. Any interpretations of other people's thoughts that we make when under stress are inherently ill conceived and hindered by our own issues. As Kant believed, it is only the judgments of the unprejudiced that should be taken into account, so mindfulness is a necessary practice for all those who want to better read minds.

Next, we have to determine who it is whose mind we want or need to read. If we come out of the gates swinging, so to speak, trying to tell what is going on within everyone's inner lives, then we are invariably bound to experience a great deal of pushback and make more than a few enemies in the process. We should go about determining our people strategically if the situation calls for it. If we are in need of a best man for a wedding, for example, it will not serve our purpose to read the minds of the women who we meet at the supermarket. This may sound like a Machiavellian line of reasoning, but we can only read so many people's minds, so we should be selective about who we try to do so to and use our powers for good.

When we have our person/people in mind, the first indicators of their characters and thinking patterns we are granted are found in their external appearances. Details like their face(s), body language, posture, and clothing should be paid attention to. Typically, a person's outward appearance is an accurate reflection of their inward life, though there are many exceptions to this rule. Many modern philosophers consider us all to be cultural constructs, always being influenced and even shaped into what we are by the culture that surrounds us. This is why we can often tell much more about a person by what they look like on the outside than many pop culture platitudes would tend to suggest that we can. What more, we are always making political statements in what we wear, consume, and associate with, so these items can act as great indicators of what we are truly like as well.

While some of the people whose minds we try to read are premeditated figures (meaning we have made up our minds beforehand to analyze them), other people just seem to jump out at us, begging for our attention by how they look, act, and seem to think. This is one of the main reasons why mind reading is always being and never becoming because the "truths" that we hold about people are constantly being shaped by the whole of people we know, within both old relationships and new. We ultimately cannot divorce our understanding of one person or group from any of the others we know. All of them our inextricably linked one to the other by our understanding as a whole.

When we see other people, there are two main categories in which our minds our perceiving our external reality: what is the person and what is not the person. While the setting that the person is within may contain insights into who the person truly is, we still need to differentiate between the person and whatever setting this might be. It is impossible to do this fully because sense perception is ultimately confused and disorganized, but once sense perception is made clearer by abstracting from its individuality and singularity (in this case separating the individual from the setting) it becomes higher order cognition. The point here is to not let other things in the background influence our own perceptions of the people we are communicating with.

With this laser-like focus given to the person we are communicating with, we can flush out any of the distracting background information that we are taking in, better enabling us to truly understand what is going on inside the person's head. When our energies become diluted by needless background worries we lose our ability to see clearly what others are thinking.

We should always make these decisions as to who to read carefully because we are constantly being shaped by those around us. The people who we spend the most time with and who we pay attention to most closely are always going to shape our characters much more than any others. Those who we read most closely should not only be the ones who offer us the most, but they should also be the ones who encourage us to be our best selves the most. In this way, we can become much better people merely by following those who we most admire/ get along with.

Once we are engaged with another communicator, we need to maintain our focus on the person. This includes making eye contact: a task that most are not willing to carry through with. Around 15 seconds is the ideal amount of time to maintain eye contact with a person upon meeting them. Any more time tends to make others uncomfortable, while any less does not foster a great connection with the other.

Once this eye contact has been made we should formulate a mental image of who we have made contact with. We should take note of and remember the face of the person we have met, as well as the energy they have given off. We should let the thoughts and emotions on the person's face make an impression on us. This should be done with the same sense of openness as all the stages of this practice are, as we have to accept all of the impressions that we get from the other, whether good or bad and also cannot skim over any of these bad impressions that we get without any self-criticism.

Once we have made initial contact with the person in this more analytical manner we can start to truly read the thoughts of the other. Doing this with any justice done to the person at hand involves keeping a certain amount of receptiveness and cooperation. Conversing with another is supposed to be a two way street, on which there is a negotiated and equal dialogue among parties. Where most people run into trouble is in their proclivity toward valuing their own points above those of any others. This is where a large portion of interpersonal conflict arises, where people only want to focus on their own ideas and never think to listen to those of others.

We should typically trust and follow our own intuition while conversing with others. This requires honesty and openness, and also a fair amount of security, as we never know how much other people are trying to read us. Conversations, as we all know, tend to work best when all parties are on the same page, but without transparency, there is never any determining whether or not we are in agreement with those who we are speaking with. We are rational actors capable of defending ourselves wherever we need to do so, so we should never feel threatened moving into new conversations and relationships, even if the other parties may be working toward malevolent ends.

Allowing any thoughts to come our way from others is the only way to ensure that we are getting maximum information out of what is being said. Those who look into the bad or disagreeable thoughts here will be rewarded in the long run for doing so. To ignore the scary or dark thoughts of others is just as maladaptive as ignoring the good ones. We should avoid holding anything against the other person upon meeting them, but whatever bad things that present themselves should be looked into. It should also be noted that often times when we feel scared or uncomfortable by something it is a good indication that we are about to learn something that we do not already know. The disagreeable things that we come across usually teach us much more than do the nice things, so we should look into and feel deeply the worse thoughts of others.

Our own emotional intelligence needs to be fostered if we are going to make any attempts at reading the thoughts of others. When we cannot pinpoint our own thoughts and aspirations, as we often cannot, we are not able to pinpoint those of others. Looking at our reasoning behind the thoughts we have will enable us to solve our own problems and to then ascertain what we would like out of other people. We are always in a negotiated dialogue with others around us, always sending out signals as to how we expect to be dealt with, as well as receiving signals as to how others expect us to deal with them. When we do not know what we are thinking and what we want the former half of this dialogue is never met, and we are consequently left only with information as to what others want from us, never having asserted our own appetites and aversions.

All too many listeners listen only to respond rather than to understand. This draws back to our tendency to only take our own ideas into account while conversing with others. People are able to tell a notable difference between these two types of listeners, and putting our own responses above understanding is always a surefire way to put people off of us, often times for good. Everyone has interjections to make at all points within a conversation. Those who are less secure and more dependent upon external validation are much more likely to pay attention to their own interjections than to what is actually being said. Those who listen to others with genuine reception and curiosity, only interested in getting a clear picture of the content of what is being said, are a rare breed in a solipsistic world polluted by needless opinions and assertions, and one that is increasingly valued and sought after by all.

Listening more than we speak is another step that we can take in the same vein as the last one. While those who limit their interjections in social situations may not immediately gain the same reverence as others, these people do usually end up absorbing more information than others. Constantly speaking reduces the value of our own words. The paradox of speech is found where this desire to gain visibility through our speech by over speaking causes us to become invisible. When entering a conversation we should keep in mind that, unless we are teaching or instructing, our main job is usually to listen. While this may not seem as glamorous as speaking constantly, it does usually offer much more rewards, and while we may not gain admiration for our erudition in the short term, in the long term silence will make us wise, and we will usually appear so to others.

Most people are choosing to become less empathetic as time goes on. It is noted that this is a choice because it takes very little effort, in reality, to identify with others. Empathy is reciprocal, meaning that when we empathize with others they become much more likely to do the same with us. So many interpersonal problems are constructed merely out of conflicting parties working towards their own interests without stepping back for a second and considering what it is that the others are thinking. Mind reading is largely a game of empathy, one that rewards being able to identify with other people's qualms and work with them towards common goals. In order to empathize well, however, we need to put our own thoughts first, otherwise, we are bound to simply serve others in our relationships.

If we are going to make further progress on reading the thoughts of others we are going to have to analyze them holistically. This is where some problems will always arise because no two people are exactly the same. People are complicated, and just when we think we have figured out another fully, yet another layer of the onion that is their personality is peeled away, asking us to strip away axiomatic preconceptions and other facets of our integrated knowledge structure in order to adapt to the changes that we are met with.

One of the biggest differences that can occur between two or more people is a generational difference or one of age. All generations have (sometimes dramatically) different interpersonal styles. A generation Xer, for example, is usually going to prefer face to face contact, while a millennial will often prefer contact through social media, text, etc.

Taking a person's generation into account will help us to better conduct affairs with them. This extends to both how we should speak to them and what we should speak about. People are inclined toward nostalgia, so we will typically be better off speaking about the 1950s with a baby boomer than with a homelander. Most communication today is done via technology, so we should expect to have conversations with younger people through our devices more so than those with older people. Here we should cater to the wants of others while also ensuring that we have room for our own interests and peculiarities.

Hot buttons are another thing to keep note of, as there are very few things that will close a person up as a conversationalist quite like squishing their opinions regarding these issues that they hold convictions about so dearly. After we do so we run the risk of remaining in a conversation with a person whose opinion(s) we have squashed, which is never an ideal situation to find ourselves within. We should look for what bothers and pains others out of a desire to either avoid these topics or to render whatever aid we can muster, not to pour salt into wounds and to add insult to injury. Here again, empathy comes into play, the ability to see and understand why people feel the way they do about these topics.

The issues that we find most important are incredibly reflective of our character. When someone takes a firm stance on something we should take their opinion seriously because odds are that they have thought about the subject more than we have ourselves. Most people are surprisingly insightful, especially when it comes to issues that they feel beg their attention. It is much too easy to get caught up in the heat of the moment and to insult others for their views, but this mode of conduct does not help interpersonal connections.

Next, we should take note of the individual personalities that we are dealing with. This can be the hardest step because a personality is an incredibly complex and multifaceted construction that cannot be merely glanced over once. While first impressions usually give us pretty reliable indications of what a person is really like, we always have to delve much deeper into a person than what meets the eye if we want to determine how to conduct ourselves around them.

We have to make some concerted effort to tailor our conversational style to the personality style that we are in contact with. This entails ascertaining what a person is like fundamentally and adjusting our communication directed at them accordingly. Here the MBTI personality types can be used to our advantage. This system categorizes personalities in terms of four categories: favorite world (introversion or extraversion), information (sensing or intuition), decisions (thinking or feeling), and structure (judging or perceiving).

Extraverts tend to focus most of their energies into their outer worlds, whereas introverts prefer to introspect. People who sense usually focus only on the pure information they are given, while those who intuit usually add their own interpretations and meaning. Thinkers tend to consider consistency and logic while making decisions, while feelers look more at people involved and special circumstances. When observing the outside world, judges tend to want to get things decided whereas perceivers prefer to stay open to new information. All of these personality dimensions should be kept in mind when conversing with others because these dimensions can create large chasms between people that will have to be crossed.

Looking into the verbiage that a person uses, as well as his or her tone of voice, is a great way to gain insights into the personality of who you are speaking with. By using these tools we can dig deeper and deeper down into the understory of the other person as well as the relationship that we have with them. Without using these tools we are left blind in our search for how to better deal with the person.

Nonverbal communication should also continually be addressed. This form of communication is always taken note of when we first meet a new person, but all too many of us let this notice fall by the wayside as relationships develop. Paying continued attention to this form of communication will always give great rewards to those who choose to do so. The main areas of concern to be taken into account while observing nonverbal communication are the use of eye contact, the use of time, of touch, of voice, the use of physical appearance/environment, distance, and body language.

Encoding and decoding are the two processes used in transmitting and deciphering nonverbal language respectively. These processes can take place either consciously or unconsciously. The signals are given off while encoding are usually ones that we perceive to be universal, while those registered during decoding depend on the disposition of the encoder. Nonverbal communication is also heavily influenced by culture. We learn certain nonverbal cues, by both encoding and decoding, from a young age and continue on using most of these cues throughout our lives. Every society has its own set of nonverbal cues, but there are certain universal regulators of this type of communication applicable to all people.

An astonishing two thirds of all communication is done through nonverbal means. This means that this supposedly subordinate form of communication is, in reality, more important that verbal communication. Most of the time nonverbal cues will match the content of speech rather well, though there is often divergence in the signals produced by these two forms of communication. This divergence can be resultant of deceit, poor communicative ability, or just a lack of overall communication by the encoder. It is usually the nonverbal cues that are most accurate to follow in these cases, as 83% of what we perceive is given to us by sight, 11% by hearing, 3% by smell, 2% by touch, and 1% by taste.

It only takes one tenth of a second for someone to judge another upon meeting them and to make their first impression. First impressions are usually produced nonverbally and tend to last a long time in their effectiveness. There are both positive and negative first impressions, both of which are usually made through the presentation of the other person in terms of appearance and what he or she is saying, and through the personal prejudices of the individual being impressed upon. Though these impressions are often misleading, especially when given to the prejudiced, they are more often than not pretty accurate representations of the people giving off the impressions.

When most think of nonverbal communication, the first aspect of it that comes to mind is posture. Body posture can often tell more about what is going on inside of a person's mind than the words they speak will. These postures usually include things such as crouching, arm crossing, shoulders forward, jaw trust, legs spread, and towering. Before analyzing the body language of others we should first go over a few tips as to how to better our own body language.

Facial expressions are one of the most important factors in making first impressions. By starting a relationship off with a smile, you are associating yourself with positivity. 48 percent of Americans claim that a person's smile becomes their most memorable trait after meeting them. Sometimes excessive smiling can seem unauthentic or even arrogant but smiling authentically always tends to charm.

Not only does smiling make good first impressions more accessible, but it also is shown to decrease levels of stress hormones such as cortisol and adrenaline. Smiling is not only friendly, but it is also one of the main keys to longevity.

A proper handshake remains one of the tenants of politeness the world over. Giving a good one, however, depends on maintaining that important balance between being too firm and too soft. If a healthy medium is established than you will make much better first impressions.

Verbal introductions are the most important part of the first seven seconds spent with someone. There are plenty of common introductions in our vernacular, these include 'hello', 'nice to meet you', etc. Whichever one you use; a verbal introduction can help very much to break the silence and tension involved in meeting someone new.

A common issue that lots of people are confronted with in meeting new people is that they lack the confidence to speak clearly. Speaking timidly is not only an easy way to be overlooked but it also often leads to being taken less seriously. It has been shown that those who speak in a deeper and calmer voice are usually taken more seriously, so find a balance between whispering and screaming and you will tend to create better relationships.

Eye contact shows others that you are not only interested in what they are saying, but that you are also confident in yourself. Eye contact is also a great indicator of respect among people. It is, however, to be used in moderation though. Too much eye contact can intimidate a person or make them feel uncomfortable, while looking away may be construed as a distraction.

Body language is, more often than not, mirrored when two people are talking to one another. Your smile, for example, is mirrored by those around you by means of a specialized neuron responsible for mirroring facial expressions. This establishes between the two of you mutual understanding, connection, and trust. Other usages of positive body language are helpful as well, especially when carried out within the first seven seconds of meeting a new person.

Your attire can be a huge indicator of what you are like to a new person. If you dress in clothes that make you feel comfortable and confident people are more likely to perceive you as being that way. The opposite, however, is also true. Not only will dressing well help you to make better first impressions, but it will also improve your mood and your confidence.

In the words of Dale Carnegie, "We should be aware of the magic contained in a name and realize that this single item is wholly and completely owned by the person with whom we are dealing and nobody else." People very much enjoy hearing their own names, even more so than they usually realize. Hearing one's own name can especially stick out to people in the modern era, which is so overwhelming in its excess of names and information. Once you remember someone's name, it is always a good idea to keep calling that person by their name as this you make you seem more agreeable.

This is an aspect of life that people tend to neglect. Ask yourself what your own goals are in meeting any given new person. A clear vision of what these goals might be will give you more of an idea of how to set your tone and behave around this person. This will also make it much easier to communicate with others because you will have a better idea of what you are communicating.

No one wants to talk to a person who is not interested in what they have to say or who does not think before he or she speaks. This is why it is important to err on the side of viewing others as potential teachers and also to be precise in what you have to say. It will make others more inclined to want to talk to you if you show empathy for them and try to give them only the best of what you have to say. Showing thoughtfulness in your words or actions is one of the best ways of making a lasting impression on others.

Bad moods can make unexpectedly strong impressions on people. If you are meeting a new person but are in a bad mood for whatever reason, try your hardest to leave your negativity behind you. It is always amazing how easily negative attitudes can rub off on others around you.

# Chapter five: Cognitive psychology

      The main focus of the cognitive approach to psychology is the study of mental processes, including but not limited to thinking, creativity, problem solving, perception, memory, language use, and attention. The focus on the mental processes of humans can be seen all the way back in ancient Greece with Plato, the first philosopher on record to assert that the brain is the seat of human mental processes. Rene Descartes would later add to our understanding of the mind with his conviction that all humans are born with innate ideas, as well as with his notion of a mind-body dualism of human beings. After these two thinkers, one of the most popular debates in philosophy would become one of the notions of experiential thought (empiricism) vs. that of innate ideas (nativism). In the 19th century, George Berkeley and John Locke would argue on the side of the empiricists while Immanuel Kant would be the main proponent of the nativist view.

The next large step to be made in the field of cognitive psychology was Paul Broca's discovery of a certain area of the brain responsible for the production of language. This leap was promptly followed by a similar one in which Carl Wernicke discovered another area largely responsible for language comprehension. Both of these areas were then named after their founders and maladaptation and trauma to these areas causing disruptions to an individual's production of language or comprehension is called Broca's aphasia or Wernicke's aphasia to this day.

The 1920s to the 1950s saw a rise in the popularity of behaviorism. The first adherents of the school of thought considered things such as consciousness, attention, ideas, and thoughts to be unobservable and outside of the realm of psychological study. While the behaviorist view had its strong points, it also contained its demerits and Jean Piaget was the first notable figure of the time to go against the grain of the school and to study the intelligence, language, and thoughts of individual children and adults.

The WW2 area saw the founding of information theory, the study of the communication, storage, and quantification of information within the brain. This proved to be of more use in tracking the performance of soldiers fighting on the fronts than behaviorism, which had no explanation of how well troops would fair in combat. The development of AI would later have a profound influence on psychological thought, as many psychologists started at once to see parallels between computerized "brains" and those of humans in the areas of memory storage and retrieval. The cognitive revolution of the 1950s, initiated by Noam Chomsky, created the field of cognitive science by analyzing the production of thought processes through a multidisciplinary lens including maxims within the fields of anthropology, linguistics, and psychology.

The term "cognition" is a blanket term used to refer to all processes in which sensory input is used, recovered, stored, elaborated, transformed, and reduced. Even when these processes are bereft of sensory information they remain active, often manifesting images and sometimes hallucinations. With this broad definition, it becomes clear that cognition is involved in everything that a person does. There are, however, still different ways of analyzing thought processes that deviate from this cognitive approach, including the dynamic approach, which would analyze a subject's instincts, needs, or goals rather than his or her beliefs, remembrances, or visions when taking actions or experiences into account.

Cognitive psychology analyzes mental processes with the main objective of looking into behavior. The first mental process that cognitive psychologists take into account is that of attention, in which awareness is keenly focused on a mere subset of the perceptual information available to a person. Here irrelevant information is filtered out from the more important things going on, giving the individual greater power to analyze specific sensory input. The human brain can cognize tactile, taste, olfactory, visual, and audio information at once, but it is only when a select amount of this information is focused on that we can clarify this information.

There are two main attentional systems used within our mind: exogenous and endogenous control. Exogenous control focuses more on pop-out effects and orienting reflex, while endogenous control focuses more on conscious processing and divided attention.

Divided attention is one of the focal points of cognitive psychology. While divided attention does make information processing more difficult, we still do retain the ability to perform tasks when we have a lot on our plate, so to speak. The cocktail party effect attests to this notion, asserting that we are able to carry on conversations and pay attention to their contents in environments in which there are many more conversations taking place. The information being shadowed done, however, fall by the wayside, leaving our memory as soon as we cognize it.

The next process that cognitive psychologists look into is that of memory. There are two main types of memory: long term memory and short term, both containing their own subtypes therein. Short term memory will here be referred to as working memory, as this is the verbiage most commonly used within the field today.

Working memory, while typically used interchangeably with short term memory as a term, refers to our ability to take in information when distractions are present. This form of memory consists of a central executive burg of memory that is interconnected inextricably with a phonological loop of language, a visuospatial sketchpad of visual semantics, and an episodic buffer of short-term episodic memories. The main issue of memory is forgetting. Cognitive psychology offers us two competing solutions to this problem: decay theory which asserts that memories leave us after a while due merely to the passage of time, and interference theory which asserts that memories leave us due to their being interfered with by others pieces of information being brought in as time goes on.

Next, we have long-term memory, of which there are three main subclasses. Procedural memory is the memory used for the completion of tasks which takes place either unconsciously or requires a minimal amount of conscious effort. This type of memory contains stimulus response information that is used to perform certain tasks or routines. This type of memory makes the seemingly automated completion of tasks and routines possible. Driving a car and riding a bicycle are two great examples of actions performed with this type of memory used.

Next, we come to semantic memory. This is the type of memory wherein our more encyclopedic knowledge is found. Pieces of information that we pick up over the years through diverse sources are incorporated into our stores of this type of memory. For example, our knowledge of types of turtles in our area or what the leaning Tower of Pisa looks like would be stored in our semantic memory. The access granted to us of these pieces of information within this system of memory is dependent on a number of factors, including how recently the piece of information was gained, the level of its meaning, its frequency of access, and the number of associations that it may have with other pieces of information. We typically remember the most recent and salient of our memories, paying extra attention to the pieces of information that affect us directly and profoundly in the present moment.

Finally, episodic memory is used to store and recall autobiographical sketches that can be explicitly stated by the individual. This type of memory contains temporal memories only, such as when a person brushed his or her teeth last and when the individual purchased his or her first car. Retrieving memories from this type of memory takes more conscious effort than to do the same with memories of other types, as it is necessary to combine both temporal information and semantic memories to paint the pictures of what we are trying to find. This is, however, arguably the most important type of long term memory due to the fact that it contains bother the temporal information and the semantic memory previously mentioned.

Now we come to the process of perception. This process entails the interpretation, identification, and organization of sensory input (of propriotation, touch, sight, smell, hearing, and taste) and the reconciliation of the individual cognitive processes that go into those sensory channels. The earliest studies of this process were done by structuralists such as Edward Titchener, who attempted to reduce all of the human thought to its most basic constituent components by observing how individuals respond to sensory stimuli.

Metacognition is, broadly, the thoughts that an individual has about his or her own thoughts themselves. For example, metacognition would be used under the following circumstances: the effectiveness of a person in determining his or her own capabilities of performance of certain tasks, a person's introspective understanding or his or her own strengths and weaknesses in performing certain mental tasks, and a person's ability to employ cognitive strategies to solve problems.

Where the study of metacognition proves to be most useful is within the field of education. A student's ability to cognize objectively his or her own thinking patterns has repeated been linked to better study and learning habits. One of the main reasons for this correlational existence lies within the student's added ability to set and meet goals through self-regulation. Metacognitive tasks are a great way to ensure that students are accurately assessing the degree of their own knowledge and gaining skills in their goal setting abilities.

Some of the most common phenomena related to metacognition are Deja Vu (the feeling of repeating experience), cryptomnesia (the unconscious plagiarism of past thoughts combined with the belief of their novelty and uniqueness), the false fame effect (the making out of non-famous names to be in fact famous), the validity effect (wherein repeated exposure to statements seems to give them more validity), and imagination inflation (the imagining of an event that never in fact occurred with the confidence that it did occur increasing over time).

Dual process theory asserts that thoughts can come from two different processes. The first of these processes is implicit and unconscious and occurs automatically, while the second is explicit and conscious, occurring under controlled conditions.

Modern social psychology owes much of its knowledge to earlier studies done by cognitive psychologists. The sub-set of social psychology that is most inextricably linked with the field of cognitive psychology is that of social cognition, which studies the ways in which people store, process, and applies information regarding particular people and social situations. This sub-set helps us understand human interactions on a basis that would never have otherwise been possible.

Theory of mind, broadly, deals with the ability of an individual to attribute and understand the cognition of those around them. This theory is especially useful in the field of developmental psychology, where analyzing this ability in developing children and adolescents is essential for predicting and determining behavioral patterns being applied within social situations. Cognitive psychology intermingles with developmental psychology effortlessly because our ability to cognize asserts itself from the start of our lives. Theory of mind, on the other hand, only starts to occur around the ages of four to six, due to the fact that this is usually when a child starts to recognize that he or she has his or her own thoughts and therefore other people must have thoughts of their own. Theory of mind is essentially a form a metacognition in that it requires that we analyze our own thoughts as well as those of others.

Jean Piaget was the first developmental psychologist to prognosticate the theory of cognitive development. This theory analyzes the development of human intelligence as a person develops into an adult.

Educational psychology has also been profoundly influenced by the field of cognitive psychology. Metacognition is analyzed in educational psychology in terms of self-monitoring, which keeps track of how accurately students monitor their own performance when learning and developing new skills. This also entails the analysis of how well they apply the knowledge of their own shortcomings to better this performance.

Declarative and procedural knowledge is also analyzed in educational psychology. Declarative knowledge is more like the cumulative encyclopedic knowledge that we gain throughout the years, whereas procedural knowledge deals more with knowledge of how to perform certain tasks and or pieces of information relating to these tasks. One of the most daunting tasks that many educational psychologists face throughout their careers is getting children and adolescents to integrate declarative knowledge into their systems of procedural knowledge.

Knowledge organization is another ongoing issue in the field of educational psychology. The knowledge of how knowledge is organized and sorted in the brain gained by cognitive psychologists has greatly benefitted the field of educational psychology. This organization takes place in a series of hierarchies that prove to be of much use for educational psychologists to keep in mind in their work.

Cognitive psychology is, as the name would suggest, much more concerned with the concepts of applied psychology than cognitive science is. It is also differentiated from this field of science in that it attempts to analyze psychological phenomena. Cognitive psychologists are often in the study of how the human brain absorbs, processes, and bases decision making on the input granted to it. The information that they obtain within this study is usually kept and applied within the field of clinical psychology. This field of psychological study is unique in that it is so strongly linked with the fields of linguistics, philosophy, artificial intelligence, neuroscience, and anthropology.

We could argue that the role of cognitive science is subordinate to that of cognitive psychology. This would be justified because much (if not most) of the findings of cognitive scientists are only used within the field of cognitive psychology. Work done in this field can sometimes be of more use than any done in cognitive psychology due to the fact that cognitive scientists often perform experiments on other animals that would be considered unethical to perform on humans.

The earliest criticisms of cognitive psychology came from behaviorists, who generally disagreed with the empiricism of the field, finding it to be incompatible with the existence of mental states. The answer to this criticism was later most sharply expressed in the sub field of cognitive neuroscience, which found evidence of direct correlations between real, physiological brain activity and determinative mental states.

Another major research area within cognitive psychology is the process of categorization. This process entails the recognition, differentiation, and understanding of the substrate of objects and ourselves as subjects. This process is needed to draw differences and similarities between things in our observable reality. Where some of us start to see issues is, however, when this categorization of objects and subjects starts to make two facts within a continuum indistinguishable, causing paradoxes in contradictory statements wherever they present themselves.

Within our power of judgment sits or the ability of induction and acquisition, which allows us to lean concepts by discerning exemplars from non-exemplars. The abilities to distinguish similarities and differences between objects and to represent, classify and structure what we draw in from sensory experience is also found within our power of judgment. This power does, however, subordinate to the power of understanding, meaning that none of these abilities are possible without understanding.

Cognitive psychology also researches the area of knowledge representation and reasoning. This area of thought gives us the ability to represent information given to us from the outside world and to use this information to reason toward our own ends. The subordinate issues dealt with in knowledge representation and reasoning are propositional encoding, numerical cognition, mental imagery, media psychology, and dual-coding theories.

Language is another area researched commonly by cognitive psychologists. The acquisition of language, as well as the issues of language processing, grammar, linguistics, phonology, and phonetics, are the main areas of concern regarding language within the field of cognitive psychology. These studies often overlap with those of linguistics, but cognitive psychologists usually look more into the areas of language acquisition and processing than their counterparts.

Memory is likely to be the most commonly researched area of cognition within the field of cognitive psychology. Broadly, memory is the function of the brain by which pieces of information are stored, encoded, and retrieved when they are needed.

Age related memory loss is the most common issue concerning memory, as most of us have fair capabilities concerning memory that wane as we age. Autobiographical memory stores our recollections of our own past experiences, as its name would suggest. Childhood memory deals with childhood experiences. Constructive memory is a memory that erroneously constructs falsified recollections of past events. There is also a strong link between emotion and memory of all kinds that are researched by cognitive psychologists.

Episodic memory deals with past autobiographical events that can be recollected clearly, whereas eyewitness memory is just episodic memory that pertains to crimes or other dramatic events from a person's past. A false memory is merely an erroneous one, as its name would suggest. Flashbulb memories are short, incredibly detailed memories of past events. There are also long and short term memories and semantic memory, all of which we have gone over previously. The source-monitoring error occurs when the source of a memory is wrongfully attributed to some experience other than that which gave it birth. The psychological spacing effect can be used to our advantage when we space the repetition of our reviews of learned material in order to better remember said material. There are also many different types of memory biases that hinder our faculty of memory that will not be gone over here for the sake of brevity.

Perception is another area of great concern within cognitive psychology. Attention, object recognition, and pattern recognition is the three main areas of concern. Form perception is the most commonly studied form of perception within cognitive psychology. Psychophysics, a relatively new area of study, analyzes the relationship between the physical stimuli that we are met with and our perceptions and sensations related to them. Lastly, time sensation studies how we perceive and are affected by time.

Thinking is likely the broadest area of research within cognitive psychology. The term "thought" refers to the goal oriented flow of associations and ideas that can be driven towards reality oriented conclusions. A choice is a form of thought that follows a purposiveness presupposed by the chooser. This form of thought involved discerning the merits and demerits of options placed before us and choosing one or more of these options accordingly. The faculties of induction and acquisition used in concept formation are also forms of thought.

Decision making is the cognitive process of choosing one or more options presented to oneself, then initiating a course of action based on the choosing. Logic is inference studied systematically. A concise relation of logical support between the presuppositions made in the inference and the real conclusion has to be made in order for an inference to achieve validity. The psychology of reasoning is the scientific study of how people draw conclusions from information and make decisions based on those conclusions. Problem solving is simply the solving of issues we are faced with.

The main objective that cognitive psychologists aim to meet is the completion of models of the information processing that goes on inside a person's brain. Consciousness, memory, thinking, perception, attention, and language are the main areas of concern within this field. By completing these models, as the general idea goes, we can work with pre-established blueprints to determine how these processes are bound to take place in other individuals. The three main subcategories nested within this field are human experimental psychology (dealing primarily with issues concerning memory, attention, language, and problem solving), the approach of analogous computer information processing (including AI and computer simulations), and cognitive neuroscience (usually studying the effects of brain damage on cognition).

Around the 1950s a few developments in the psychological sciences necessitated the growth of cognitive psychology. These include but are not limited to the dissent from behaviorist psychology which placed much emphasis on external behaviors but none on the internal processes initiating these behaviors, development of newer, often more effective experimental methods, and new comparisons being drawn between the human mind and computer processing of information. Whether cognitive psychology answered the questions of the times surrounding these issues most effectively or not, behaviorism was becoming an extinct approach, driven out by its own antiquated methodology.

The rise of cognitive psychology was inversely proportional to the fall of some of the more erroneous approaches to psychology at the time. This field shook off the chaff of conditioned behavior and many psychoanalytic approaches of the time.

Behaviorists were typically averse to the study of the mind's internal processes because they believed that these processes could not be objectively observed and measured. Cognitive psychologists responded to this reluctance by observing and studying the mental processes of organisms, seeing doing so as an essential part of learning more about them. Mediational processes between stimulus and response within organisms were the first specific objects of study for cognitive psychologists, and remain paramount objects of study within the field to this day.

Cognitive psychologists did parallel behaviorists in that they employed controlled, objective, and scientific methods to pursue their ends. The only difference between the two groups here is that cognitive psychologists were using these methods to analyze the mental processes of organisms, whereas behaviorists were not.

Our brains are similar to computers in how they transform, store, and retrieve information (which should come as no surprise when considering that humans program computers). A clear sequence is shown in most models of information processing. The cognitive processes of attention and memory usually have the clearest of these sequences.

The analysis of stimuli is usually found within input processes. Storage processes within the brain can code and sometimes manipulate the perception of stimuli. Finally, output processes legislate our responses to stimuli.

In the late 1950s and early 1960s, the cognitive approach became the most widely accepted approach in the field of psychology, revolutionizing the way we perceive internal cognitive processes. The work of Piaget and Tolman is the main reason for this reality.

Tolman is considered by most today to be a soft behaviorist. His study of purposive behaviors in organisms, however, diverged from the behaviorist paradigm stating that learning was the product of the relationship between stimuli and responses. Tolman asserted to the contrary that learning stemmed from the relationships between stimuli amongst one another. The term he coined to refer to these relationships was "cognitive maps".

It was not until the arrival of the computer that cognitive psychology would gain the metaphor and terminology it needed to properly investigate the mind. This arrival gave psychologists the opportunity to draw analogies between the human mind and the processes of a computer, the latter being, on the whole, much more simple and easily understood. This analogy hearkens back to that one drawn by Plato in his Republic between the individual components of a state and the human mind. What more, this analogy also became the focal point of the Leibnitz-Searle argument. Essentially, a computer encodes information, changes it, stores it, uses it, and finally produces an output of some sort.

This computerized model of information processing was observed by cognitive psychologists who believed that the same or a similar model was used within the human brain. This approach is, however, rooted in a few key assumptions: that information from our external environment is processed by a series of processes (including perception, attention, memory, etc.), that transformation and alteration of these processes occur in systematic ways, that research is supposed to aim at specifying these processes and systems, and that computer information processing resembles that of humans.

The behaviorist approach offers us that we can observe and study the external (stimulus and response) processes that we are met with, but our observations under this approach are limited only to these external processes. The cognitive approach, to contrast, asserts that we can observe and study the internal processes going on within the mind. This approach studies the mediational relationships between stimulus/input and response/output.

The behaviorist approach works in a linear progression within the following frame: stimulus from the environment, a "black box" which cannot be studied, and response behavior. The cognitive approach follows a similar progression: input from the environment, a mediational process in the mental event, and output behavior. As we can see, aside from differences in verbiage, the main difference between these two progressions is found in their transient steps: while the behaviorist approach only offers us a black box of ignorance as to internal mental processes, the cognitive approach investigates the mediational processes occurring within mental events.

These mediational processes are so called because they are meant to go in between the stimulus and the response of the mental event. This response could include processes such as problem solving, attention, memory, perception, etc. Whatever they might be, these processes come about after the stimulus has been met and before the behavioral response is found.

The causal relationships between all of these mental processes in some instances beg teleological judgments regarding their parts. Here we see clear, linear paths of purposive behaviors following stimuli and subsequent mediational processes.

Where the behaviorist model is said to lack here is in the knowledge of these intermediary mediational processes that go on within the mind. It is clear to us today that in order to understand behavioral psychology we must first understand these mediational processes. To do otherwise would be in many ways to put the cart before the horse.

It was Kohler's 1925 book *mentality of the apes* that started the popular split from the behaviorist model within the psychological sciences. In this book Kohler investigated the more insightful behaviors of animals, founding a little known field by the name of Gestalt psychology in the process. The terms input and output, so commonly used in cognitive psychology, were first introduced into the field in Norbert Wiener's 1948 book *Cybernetics: or control and communication in the animal and the machine*. Tolman's 1948 observations on cognitive maps done on rats in mazes were the first study to prove that animals have internal representations of behaviors.

It was *The magical number 7 plus or minus 2* of 1958 by George Miller that ultimately saw the birth of cognitive psychology. The general problem solver developed by Newell and Simon was the next great discovery within the field. In 1960, the Center for Cognitive Studies was finally founded by Miller and cognitive developmentalist Jerome Bruner. Ulric Neisser's 1967 publication of "*Cognitive psychology*" marks the definitive birth of the cognitive approach. Shiffrin and Atkinson's 1968

Multi Store model became the first processing model of memory. Today, at last, cognitive psychology is seen as a highly influential field throughout all areas of psychological study (biological, behaviorist, social, developmental, etc.).

A cognitive psychologist would be helpful to speak to for anyone who might be experiencing the following issues: a psychological issue that may need cognitive therapy methods to mitigate or exterminate, brain trauma that may need treatment, sensory and or perceptual issues, a speech or language disorder (more types of therapy would be needed in this case, with cognitive methods being supplementary), memory related problems such as Alzheimer's disease, dementia, or memory loss, or learning disabilities.

In essence, nearly anyone who has or is experiencing issues concerning mental processes will necessarily benefit from cognitive psychological therapy. Many feel that cognitive psychology is an erudite and impractical field of study that has much more utility within the classroom than without, but everyone has mental processes, so everyone can benefit from this area of research. Having a cognitive psychologist working for and with us will give us a more objective, scientific perspective on the mental processes we have that we may not be aware of or may be interpreting unscientifically.

One of the most stealthy adversaries of our own wellbeing is negative thinking patterns. These thinking patterns are so destructive because we usually cannot tell just how distorted they are, which enables them to legislate our thought processes without our conscious awareness. Having another perspective on our own internal mental processes is arguably the only surefire way to keep these negative patterns from controlling the rest of our minds. Negative ruminations often lead to increased stress, self-sabotaging, pessimism, and even learned helplessness after a while is we are not careful.

Once these negative thinking patterns have taken their hold over our psyches they cannot necessarily be removed. Our best option is to then replace these patterns with better, more optimistic and rational ones. For instance, a schema that is telling a person repeatedly things like "you are not worthy" or "you will never meet the standards" should be responded to with one that tells him or her things like "you have intrinsic worth" or "these standards are your own". The negative thinking patterns, as well as the rational responses to their interjections, are indeterminate and depend on the individual. All the same, the basic goal is to replace the thoughts that do not assist us or do not push us forward as individuals with ones that do. Here some self therapy could be utilized. Whenever we have a thought or a series of thoughts that our executive minds do not agree with, we should record and analyze these thoughts, editing them and replacing them with healthier, more rational ones. Doing so will change our modes of thinking and enable us to become more rational, intrinsically motivated people.

Cognitive psychology could be considered the final purpose of psychology, the one to which all other subfields are subordinate. Everything that we know of, we know of because of our ability to cognize. Without analyzing our mental processes we are leaving ourselves in the dark as to what is really going on in and outside of us.

# Chapter six: Modes of persuasion

We come at last to what is likely the most useful portion of our book. Modes of persuasion, also known as rhetorical appeals or ethical strategies, are rhetorical devices used to classify a speaker's appeal to his or her audience. These modes are called Eros, pathos, logos, and Kairos. Aristotle considered persuasion to be merely a form of demonstration, as we are most fully persuaded by the things that we perceive as having been demonstrated. It could logically follow that the more or less we demonstrate something, the more or fewer others will be persuaded of it within proportion.

There are three main kinds of spoken word persuasion: persuasion due to a perceived credibility of the speaker at the time of the speech, persuasion of the hearers due to their own emotions, and persuasion achieved through speech when truth or apparent truth is arrived at by arguments suited to the case in question.

Ethos is broadly defined as either the appeal to authority or to the speaker's credibility. In order to bolster ethos a speaker must convince the audience of his or her own credibility, often appealing to other sources of authority in the process. People employ various means of doing this, including but not limited to being or becoming a notable figure in the field in question, such as a professor, doctor, or expert, learning and demonstrating a mastery of the vernacular of the field in question, and introducing or producing proven experts in the field.

Without these broad criteria met, a speaker will generally have trouble gaining and fostering a sense of credibility or ethos. Without being an expert in the field in which he or she is speaking on, or without the necessary vocabulary and or appeal to other sources of authority, a speaker will typically lose any sense of credibility in the eyes of his or her audience, usually causing the individual to lose his or her sense of intrinsic credibility, thus starting a causal loop of the loss of overall credibility and potency as a speaker.

Ethos could be considered persuasion by character or credibility. Trustworthiness is usually the most important trait that a person can display in order to foster ethos. We tend to see those who are more trustworthy as also being more credible, as while we may not know what they are going to tell us, we are more assured that it is going to be the truth. It would necessarily follow here that in order for someone to gain ethos, he or she must become more trustable. Aristotle offers us three explicit qualities that a person must display in order to become a more trustworthy individual: good sense, good moral character, and a good will.

Good sense is found only in rational and responsible thinkers. We tend to trust those with good sense much more than we do others. Those with good sense are almost always calm, cool, and collected in times of stress and confusion. Those people are usually seen as trusted and reliable professionals within their fields of work. Good sense is associated with trustworthiness because those who have it are impelled more by logic and rationality than others without it are. With good sense, a speaker is also able to read a crowd better and to deliver messages that are more grounded in reality.

Good moral judgment was another area in which Aristotle placed lots of emphases. It is commonly said that character is what we do when no one is looking. The same is true for morality. Aristotle thought that having this sense of moral judgment was crucial to developing the art of persuasion.

Finally, good will is the state in which a person truly has our own best interests in mind. Without this will there is no clear direction within a person's mind as to where things should go or even how they should ideally be. If a speaker shows no knowledge or regard for the interests of the whole that he or she is speaking to then rapport will never be built. While a person's ethos is probably less affected by a lack of good will than by a lack of any of the other two goods, people are still put off by this absence because they will not be sure whether or not the speaker is truly on their side. It is only, as Aristotle asserts, with these three qualities that a person can be more trustworthy and gain ethos.

Pathos may be a more powerful mode of persuasion because it is dependent on a speaker's ability to appeal to the emotions of the audience. From this root word the words empathy, pathetic, and sympathy are formed. Using the common tactics of metaphor, simile, and overall passionate delivery pathos can be gained by the speaker. Often, even simple claims asserting things to be unjust are enough to appeal to the emotions of speakers. This mode of persuasion is incredibly effective when used with others but usually falls apart when used as a standalone. There are one main criterion that a speaker needs to meet in order to gain pathos though; he or she needs to deliver a message that is in agreement with some underlying values of the readers or listeners.

To gain pathos, a speaker may home in on any emotions he or she feels to be of use to tap into. These include happiness and optimism, but also include more negative emotions such as fear and anxiety. Whatever the emotions might be, a speaker with a sensitivity to the audience's emotions gains rapport with ease by speaking to people about what they find most salient.

Our adoption of beliefs and viewpoints is largely dependent upon our immediate emotions. A good speaker not only knows how to exalt certain emotions but also how to eliminate certain others. In order to get people angry about a cause, a good speaker will explain the qualms behind not following that cause. Likewise, if a crowd of people is angry about gas prices, a good speaker will calm them down and give them the assurance that they will continue to be able to get around. A persuasive person keeps in mind what others are concerned about, and offers them solutions to their problems.

When used within speeches and writings, pathos is often played on the audience's imagination and aspirations regarding future events. Persuasive thinkers are not only able to predict and speak to present emotions but are also able to convey some sort of an image of what the future could be like under their vision. Without this emphasis placed on the teleological purposiveness of what the persuader is thinking, the persuaded is left with no determinative course of action to follow and is thus destined to become unpersuaded.

While a certain amount of ethos has to be secured in order for a speaker to be listened to, this ethos is often downplayed and is put in a role subordinate to pathos. When pathos is the main mode used we often start to see less control within speech and writing and more appeal to the base and often irrational emotions. William Cullen Bryant saw this as an alright happening, claiming that anyone speaking out of righteousness will give to the world an offering that will outweigh any amount of errors that they bring with it.

Aristotle offers us some of the basic dualities of emotion in book 2 of his *rhetoric:*

Anger vs. calm

People tend to get angry when we show contempt towards, shame, or act spitefully against them. Contempt is here defined as the treating of things or people that others value as unimportant. Acting with spite is keeping others from getting what they want just to harm them. Shame is given when we discredit others in some way. Doing the opposite of these things, such as leaving things and people in their own value, holding others in esteem, and letting others have what they want, will keep people calm.

Friendship vs. hatred

It is those who act without selfishness in order to achieve what is best for us who we choose to be friends with. We show hatred towards those who are either selfish or who work towards harmful ends. Contingents are only formed among people who have common interests in mind. We divide our world into those who work with us (friends) and those who do not (foes).

Fear vs. confidence

We are fearful only of the things that we perceive to be able to bring us harm or suffering. When we do not perceive these dangers to exist, or have means of combating them, we instead feel confident. The confidence deriving from our perceived ability to combat danger is the more reliable of the two because any confidence derived from a lack of danger intimates danger in the future.

Shame vs. shameless

We feel shame when we have been discredited for displaying what Aristotle called moral badness, such as being cowardly, arrogant, avaricious, or mean. We feel shameless when we are either indifferent to or contemptible of other's perceptions of our moral badness. Shame is the concept of moral badness (real or perceived) attached to the concept of self-consciousness. Shamelessness is this concept divorced from self-consciousness.

Kind vs. unkind

We are perceived as being kind when we help others for their own sake. We are perceived as unkind when we either neglect to help others or help them merely for our own sake. Kindness is found in those who keep the interests of those who they are helping in mind. Unkindness is found in those who either do not help others or who do so for their own gains.

Pity vs. indignation

We feel pity for those who are suffering in ways and calibers that we perceive to be unproportionally to aptness. On the other hand, we feel indignation when we see others doing well and feel that they do not deserve it. Pity is felt when we see someone suffer more than is necessary, while indignation is felt when we see someone get more than their character is deserving of, or so we think.

Envy vs. emulation

Envy is felt when we see another who we consider our equal come across a good fortune. This is more keenly felt when we feel that we are entitled to the same good fortune or when we no longer see ourselves as equal to that person as a result of the fortunate circumstances. Envy stems from selfishness in that it does not offer that we may live vicariously through the other individual. We are most envious of those who we perceive to be more fortunate than us because every person wants to believe that he or she is equal to all others.

Emulation is felt when we see another who has good fortune and feel that we can achieve a similar fortune. Here we have the same stimuli as that which causes envy, but our mediational response is more constructive and positive. Aristotle considered, like most would, emulation to be the better of these two feelings because while envious people often wish the more fortunate person to have less, emulative people merely strive to achieve more. Envy is the perception of inequality with the concept of dislike towards those with more, while emulation is the same perception with the concept of self efficacy.

The concept of a human being necessarily includes that of emotion. Emotions are never right or wrong, they are only rational or irrational. Sometimes, for instance, fear and anger are the only rational responses to external realities, while at other times serenity and happiness are called for. A good persuader knows the ins and outs of the emotions of others, whether they be rational or irrational. With this knowledge, a persuader can exalt the emotions he or she wants to in other individuals, and curtail all others.

Logos is, broadly, an appeal to logic. The term logic actually derives from this one. There is generally some sort of thesis that a speaker is trying to communicate when speaking. Logic, in part, refers to the facts and figures supporting these theses, in this case. Having logos tends to beget greater ethos for a speaker because the information makes the speaker seem more knowledgeable to his or her listener(s). While logos can be incredibly useful, it can also be harmful and misleading, depending on the content of the information and its relationship with the subject at hand. Often, mis contextualized, falsified, and or inaccurate information leads listeners astray, causing them to leave the speaker and causing the speaker to lose ethos.

Aristotle tells us of three main methods of logical persuasion:

Deductive argument

In its initial stage, a sound, logical argument will put forth a series of axiomatic premises. These statements are perceived to be either true or false. From these premises, we can lead ourselves to conclusions. If a conclusion were said to be true given that all of its axiomatic premises were also said to be true then the argument would be considered valid. If all of these premises are true and the argument is said to be valid then it is also, by definition, sound. These arguments are what is known as deductive arguments. Within these arguments, the notions of validity and soundness are defined and observed from premises to conclusions. These are good arguments because they use easily intelligible logic throughout their courses.

Inductive argument

If from our initial premises, we instead find conclusions that are not necessarily but likely to be true then we are making inductive arguments. These arguments exist with the concept of uncertainty and some amount of guesswork. The strength or weakness of an inductive argument is found only in the likelihood of its conclusions to follow its premises. A cogent inductive argument is one in which all of its premises are, in fact, found to be true.

Abductive argument

An abductive argument is arrived at when we collect a set of data and then proceed to formulate a conclusion based on that data. This conclusion should always explain the data set in question. Like deductive arguments, the validity and soundness of these arguments are dependent upon the truth behind the conclusions.

Finally, Kairos refers to time and place. This mode is often used to instill a sense of urgency within the minds of the listeners, urging them to act on events as they happen.

In addition to the Aristotelian modes of persuasion, there are also numerous contemporary methods that could be used to our advantage. Though the Aristotelian modes are evergreen in their applicability, people are always coming up with new ways to persuade others, ways that are usually meant to appeal more to the people of the time.

Mimicry is one of the most surefire methods of persuasion. We tend to be much more receptive to messages when they are delivered by people who speak, think, and act as we do. Using mimicry will almost invariably boost rapport, make others like us more, and make us seem more agreeable all around. When trying to persuade others we should always take note of how they are acting and speaking, and mirror these characteristics as much as possible in order to foster a sense of kinship with us in their minds. This will put us on the same ground as them, so to speak, ensuring them that we share common interests with them and are willing to work with them to pursue these interests.

The Ellsberg Paradox was discovered in 1961 in a series of experiments conducted by Daniel Ellsberg. In these experiments, participants were told that they needed to choose between two urns to draw a ball from, the first containing 100 red and black balls with no certain proportion between the two colors, the second with exactly 50 red balls and 50 black ones. There reward was $100 if they chose the correct color, $0 if they did not. The vast majority of subjects drew from the second urn with the determinate proportion of colors.

These experiments show that we are naturally prone to avoid risk and uncertainty whenever possible. While we may benefit more from taking bets on uncertainties at times, it remains our natural proclivity to stick to certain, concise probabilities wherever we find them, even when our payoffs are shown to be less for doing so.

Social influence, or social proof, refers to our being affected by the thoughts, emotions, and behaviors of others. We are impressed upon by this sort of influence largely unconsciously, which is why it is often difficult to discern what we are doing out of our own interests from what we are doing as a result of this influence. Here the question asserts itself: to what extent are we merely the products of those around us? Most people can be analyzed as a collection of their immediate social influences.

No matter how independently minded we happen to be, we do crave external validation in order to make our thinking patterns seem "normal" to us. The people who we most admire end up being the highest authorities as to how we should think, feel, and behave, whether we like or realize it or not.

Reciprocity is another assistant of persuasion. When we receive things from others, whatever they might be, we usually feel the urge to reciprocate. When we feel this urge it compels us to appease the other, making us much more likely to be persuaded by the individual. When we give others things we are not only compelling them to reciprocate but are also making them much more likely to work with us in the future. People need an incentive of some sort in order to work towards our ends. There must be some way in which a person can gain from working with us. By doing favors and giving others things we are giving them this incentive, and urging them to reciprocate and do the same for us. We are, however, affected by experiences in an inverse proportion to their temporal distances from us, so when we do things for other people they will usually feel more compelled to reciprocate right afterwards, and this compulsion will only wane with the passage of time.

The hot hand fallacy is another phenomenon that we can use to our advantage. This is a fallacy by which people lead themselves to believe that since they happen to be finding immediate successes they will continue to do so indefinitely. While success does often beget success, life is ultimately chaotic and random and vicissitudes tend to present themselves when we least expect them to. The fallacy's modus operandi is found within the (presumptively false) perception of control that it gives us.

People are much likely to be persuaded of their future successes when they are experiencing successes. Again, the closer an experience is to us temporally, the more we are affected by it. This affection extends to our perceptions, which in this case implies that more recent successes will cause us to believe that we will have better futures. In order to persuade someone by taking advantage of this fallacy, we should lead them to believe that they are currently experiencing success, and continue to press that things are only looking up for them.

A sense of commitment and consistency will cause us to stick with the things that we choose, whatever these things might be. Whatever choices we happen to make in life, it is within our nature to stick to these choices until they show themselves to be faulty ones, if they ever do so. Along these veins that we carve for ourselves, we will travel until the change becomes necessary.

If we are trying to persuade others, we can use their sense of commitment to our advantage by first getting them to agree to smaller things, and eventually working them into bigger and bigger commitments as time goes on. People are put off by being granted too much responsibility at once. We instead prefer to ease ourselves into things by taking time to transition into them. Persuasion is, in part, a game of small asks, each one building on top of the last, leading to the greater and greater commitment between parties.

When making a decision we tend to rely all too heavily on the first pieces of information that we come across. This tendency is called anchoring and it is considered fallacious because it causes us to graze over other useful pieces of information that could help us with our decision making.

Once an anchor has been set, a bias towards its idea is also set. From this, it would necessarily follow that people are much more likely to be persuaded of something when an initial anchoring towards it has been made. If we are trying to convince someone to make a certain decision then we are going to need to give them some initial piece of information from which they can base their further decisions.

Next, simply liking another person makes us much more receptive to them. One of the greatest proponents of persuasiveness is simple likability. We are never positively influenced by those we do not like, regardless of their character. We seek to squash these people's opinions whenever we come across them and are never persuaded by the things they say as a result. In order to get a person on our side, we have to treat them in a way that causes them to like us, because without their doing so no sense of comradery can be fostered, and without any sense of comradery we will never be able to persuade them of anything.

Being friendly with others is probably the best way to get them to like us. Remembering to smile and remaining light hearted around others will make people feel more comfortable around us, opening up the door to more friendly and amiable conversations.

Sensory words should always be taken note of when trying to convince others. These words are some of the most powerful ones that we use, and people are likely more affected by these words than by any others. Words with connotations to sensory stimuli that people find agreeable can be used to convince people often without their knowing. These words are more than just words to those who hear them, they are real, tangible experiences associated with sensory experiences, so using these words wisely can have a surprisingly powerful effect on the decision making processes of those who hear them.

We also have a bias towards authority. The thoughts and opinions of authority figures are often regarded as much more valuable than they really are. We are socialized from a young age to respect authority figures and take what they say seriously. This is why the things these people say are listened to more than the things other people say. Here is where ethos remains important. In order to be listened to, not to mention to be persuasive, we have to convince our audience that we are some sort of authority on what we are talking about.

The Ikea effect is a phenomenon by which people tend to value things that they have assembled more highly than things that have come to them preassembled. We take pride in whatever it is that we produce, and consider these products to be better and more valuable than those of any others. Giving people a sense of participation in whatever it is that we are proposing to them will make them much more receptive to our ideas because they will feel as though they are a part of something that gives them a say.

People like to have options and to feel as though they are in control of what options they pursue. When we make our premises and arguments seem more customizable to others, they will identify more with what we are saying because we are encouraging something of a negotiated dialogue to take place between ourselves and them. This sense of oneness can make people much more likely to follow us wherever we decide to go intellectually.

# Chapter seven: Controlling emotions

The workplace tends to be one of the most difficult places to control emotions. No matter how hard you try, those difficult days are always bound to come up. In your personal life, your reactions to stressful situations are much freer, but in the workplace, your reactions are subject to the scrutiny of your coworkers. Any emotional outbursts while working cannot only damage your professional reputation and productivity, but they can even get you fired.

Under normal circumstances, it is usually easy to maintain composure in the workplace, but under more stressful circumstances, such as staff layoffs, budget cuts, and department changes, staying calm can prove difficult, if not impossible. Under these circumstances, however, it becomes even more important to keep your temper, as bosses typically consider the demeanor of their employees when deciding who gets laid off. You have complete freedom and how you react to certain situations, but that freedom comes with responsibility, especially in the workplace.

It may seem easy to decide how you're going to react in certain situations with hindsight, but it is always advisable to explore techniques in dealing with these situations and emotions. Here we will discuss many negative emotions associated with employment, as well as many methods of coping with these emotions.

The most commonly reported negative emotions among workers are as follows:

Worry/ nervousness, frustration/ irritation, dislike, anger/ aggravation, disappointment/ unhappiness

And now we will get into some strategies in dealing with these unhealthy emotions.

*Worry/ nervousness*

These are two of the most unpleasant and unhealthy emotions on the spectrum, and, unfortunately for workers, these two plague virtually every workplace. This anxiety can stem from a number of sources: fear of getting laid off, social problems, low salaries, large workload, etc., And be compounded with problems at home, or with family or friends by many. A small amount of stress can be a productive thing, but once it becomes chronic anxiety, health problems start to occur. Here are some tips on how to avoid excessive anxiety:

Break cycles of worry
Do not Surround yourself with anxiety. If you can foresee needless anxiety stemming from a situation or a conversation, avoid that anxiety. Try to

minimize the number of anxiety inducing things that you have to deal with.

Try deep breathing exercises
These help primarily to slow down your breathing and heart rate. There are all sorts of different deep breathing exercises that you can learn about on the internet. For one, there is cyclical breathing, with in breaths for 4 seconds followed by holding for 4 seconds, and then out breaths for 4 seconds followed by holding for 4 seconds. When doing these exercises, it is important to focus on your breathing and nothing else. In addition to these exercises, there are other physical relaxation exercises that will help reduce workplace stress, including progressive muscle relaxation.

Focus on improving the situation
Whatever it is worrying you in regards to work, brainstorming solutions and making attempts at them will help reduce your anxiety greatly. Doing these things will also make you a more valuable asset to your company.

Journal your worries down
Simply writing down the things that bother you will do a lot to alleviate the anxiety surrounding them. This technique also helps to curtail sleep problems and nightmares, as worries that we write down during the day don't typically bother us by night. Once these are written down, you can then schedule times to deal with these issues. Before that time

comes, let these issues leave you and go about your day. When that time comes, make sure to perform proper risk analysis before putting any plans into place.

Worry and nervousness can decrease self-confidence and lead to health complications. it is always important to trail these negative emotions away and remain confident and secure.

*Frustration/irritation*

Frustration is more often than not caused by the feeling of being trapped or stuck at a point which you want to get out of, but cannot. This feeling can be caused by a number of things, especially at work. A colleague blocking a project of yours, a boss too disorganized to catch a meeting on time, or a phone call held out longer than necessary are just a few examples that come to mind. Frustration, whatever its causes, should always be dealt with quickly because when it is not it can accumulate into anger and other even more negative emotions.

There are, however, many ways of dealing with this awful emotion, a few of which are listed below:

Stopping to evaluate
The best thing to do when feelings of frustration arise is to stop what you are doing and take time to evaluate them. Writing your frustrations down in this stage can help very much. After this is done,

think of some positive aspects of your current situation. This will improve your mood and reduce further frustration.

Look for positive things
Again, finding silver linings in a frustrating situation will make you see the events unfolding in a new light. This change in your thinking will improve your mood, among other things. If it is a person who is causing you frustration than keep in mind that it is probably not personal, and if it is an event or situation, than it can probably be solved. Try to move on from this step as much as possible.

Recall the last time you felt frustrated
If you can remember the last thing that you were frustrated about than you can probably remember how that thing eventually resolved itself. Looking at things with hindsight, they always work out fine. You can also probably recall that your feelings of frustration did not do much to help you in that last situation, so to assume that they are helping you this time around would not be very prudent. Perspective is everything, and so many issues lose so much of their stature when seen through different angles.

*Dislike*

Dislike for certain coworkers is inevitable, and when it pops up, it seldom goes away. We all have to work with people who we dislike at one point or another, so when these people arrive, it is important to take steps towards dealing with them responsibly. Some of the best things that you can do in these situations are to:

Show respect
You are never obligated to get along with everyone you work with, but you are, in many ways, obligated to show them all respect. When these situations arise, pride and ego are two things which you should set aside, even if the other party(s) are not willing to. This will allow you to come out of the experience with your dignity intact, whatever the outcomes may be.

Be assertive
If a coworker is rude or unprofessional with you, do not be afraid to tell them so. If you do so with certainty and fairness, they might be inclined to change some of their attitudes and behaviors in the future.

*Anger/aggravation*

Anger is arguably the most destructive emotion contained in a human. This is especially true when the anger is out of control in the workplace. It is also an emotion which most of us do not handle very well. As far as work is concerned, there is typically very little room for anger, which is problematic because much of it then gets taken home with us. Controlling this emotion is one of the most important steps in keeping any given job, especially for those who have difficulties with this. Some tips in dealing with this emotion are listed below:

Watch for the early signs of anger
No one else can detect when your anger is building up quite like you can, so detecting it early is your own responsibility. As was mentioned before, you decide how to react to situations, so if you react in anger, no one holds accountability for that happening.

When anger arises, take a break from what you are doing
When you start to get angry, closing your eyes and trying the aforementioned deep breathing exercises can help you hugely. These actions will do a lot to interrupt your angry thoughts and help to put your mind back on a more positive, relaxed pathway, reducing irrational statements and decisions made.

Picture yourself when you get angry
Imagining how you look and behave will usually give you some well needed perspective on the situation at hand. For example, if you have the urge to shout at a coworker, think about what you would look like doing so: flustered, mean, and demanding. With that imagery in mind, it is easy to see that you would not be a good coworker in making that decision.

*Disappointment/unhappiness*

Disappointment and unhappiness are two of the more pullulated emotions in modern workplaces. These two are almost equal to anger in their unhealthiness, in fact, unhappiness may be more unhealthy. These can also have detrimental impacts on your productivity, as they can leave you feeling exhausted and drained, and also less inclined to take risks in the future. Here are some steps that can be taken to curtail the effects of these awful emotions.

Consider your mindset
Try to always keep in mind that things will not always go your way. If they did, then life would become prosaic and meaningless. It is, sometimes, the adversity and the suffering that give life its meat. Do not try to avoid these things, the answer to these problems lies within the willingness to confront them.

Set and adjust your goals
Disappointment can often stem from neglecting to reach a goal. This rarely means, however, that the goal is no longer reachable though. It is natural to feel disappointment in these situations, but you must always find the willpower to pick yourself back up. You could, for example, keep your goal, but just make a small change. Anything that will help you to get past the disappointments that you face.

Record your thoughts

One method for dealing with negative emotions is to write them down. When you feel unhappy or disappointed, try writing down what is bothering you, and be specific about your concerns. Is it your job that is bothering you? A coworker? Do you have too heavy of a workload? Writing these concerns down will help you to single out what exactly is bothering you and how you can improve on these areas of concern. Remember that you always have more powers than you think in improving a situation.

Remember to smile
Forcing a smile onto your face can actually make you feel happier and relieve stress. In addition, this activity also releases the neurotransmitters dopamine, endorphins, and serotonin, which all lower heart rate and blood pressure. The endorphins released also act as natural painkillers and the serotonin acts as a natural antidepressant. Smiling will also make you look more attractive to those around you, further bettering the relationships you have with your coworkers.

Now that the main emotions that have adverse effects on most workers have been covered, let's take a look at some more strategies of dealing with these:

*Compartmentalize your stressors*

Try to keep stress and baggage from work and home in those respective places. You can use mental techniques, such as imagining the stressors locked away in a box for the time being. If you do not try to compartmentalize these issues, then waters will get very muddied up in your personal life and things will become very complicated.

*Identify your own self talk*

Relay to yourself what you tell yourself. By doing this, you may find yourself repeating thoughts and phrases to yourself that are not necessarily true or helpful. Try to identify your own thoughts that may be misleading or based on thinking errors. Doing this will help you move on from some of your worse points and attitudes into a more productive and expansive mindset.

*Identify and accept your emotion*

There is virtually nothing you can do to control an emotion that you are not even willing to come to terms with having. It is like denying the existence of a spider right in front of your eyes, the spider will just get bigger and bigger until it is all that you can see. In identifying what emotion(s) you are having and accepting that they are a natural part of life, you are taking lots of power away from them. In doing this, you are also becoming a greater solver of your own problems.

*Affirm your rights*

There are many places in life, work especially, where you are bound to feel like you have no rights and no control over what happens to you. By identifying your rights and your powers, you are giving yourself some perspective on the things that are in and out of your control. After taking some time to do this, you may find that you are much more powerful than you think you are. This will improve your mood and your self-confidence to affirm these rights that you have.

*Communicate strategically*

Anyone can drone on about the things that they do not like, but it takes skill and grit to actually get things done to fix all their problems. When you are trying to communicate with others, especially disagreements, It is always important to be precise in your language. This will allow you to communicate your qualms more effectively, and it will also decrease the chance of having misunderstandings and heated arguments. When trying to get a point across, try to come into the situation with some idea of what you want to get accomplished and your probability of having a productive conversation will increase dramatically. If others reply emotionally, let them vent and be understanding. You may learn more from them than they will from you. Ask for more details as well and the two of you will probably come closer to an understanding because of it.

*Be objective*

Try to look at whatever is bothering you from both analytic and synthetic approaches. An analytic approach will help you understand the one issue more in depth and with more clarity, while a synthetic approach will help you understand the issue within the class of all of your possible issues. It is important to look into things with depth and focus, but seeing things as parts of your whole understanding will help you to make connections and find out why these certain things bother you through free associations.

Emotions are never right or wrong, they are only felt. There is no shame in feeling emotions unless of course, the emotion is a shame. Emotions will always come and go and are always wiser than the ego. Each one of us, however, has freewill in how we react to life's vicissitudes. Controlling emotions is not always easy, in fact, sometimes it becomes nearly impossible. But this skill is just like any other in that it can be improved with practice and diligence.

# Chapter eight: Social engineering and leadership

The importance of social engineering and leadership are often underestimated by contemporary thinkers. Most people are so absorbed in manipulating and taking down hierarchical structures that they neglect to figure out how to manifest themselves within these structures. Whether you have a proclivity towards leadership or not, it still remains important to have a working knowledge of leadership and how it works among groups of people.

Leaders, above all else, help themselves and others in making steps towards doing the right things. In doing this they build an inspiring vision, set direction, and create new possibilities. Leadership is, in part, about mapping out the route to your team's successful future. It is challenging, but also exciting, dynamic, and inspiring. Setting the direction of the pack is not the only responsibility of a leader though. They are also obligated to guide their people in these directions in a smooth and efficient way. This may be the more challenging skill which takes more time to develop.

This chapter and its tips on the process of leadership will be based on the 'transformational model' of leadership proposed by James MacGregor

Burns and further developed by Bernard Bass. This model more so focuses on bringing about change through visionary leadership than the normative managerial processes designed to maintain the current performance of given groups.

**An overview of leadership**

The following are a few traits of an effective leader:

1. Succeeds in creating an inspiring vision of the future
2. Inspires and motivates people to engage with that vision
3. Manages the delivery of the vision
4. Builds and coaches a team, so that it becomes more effective in meeting the vision

Effective leadership requires all of these traits working together with one another. Next, it would be helpful to explore each one of these elements in greater detail.

*Succeeds in creating an inspiring vision of the future*

In the workforce, a vision that a boss prognosticates needs to be a convincing, realistic, and attractive depiction of the situation that you want to be in in the future. This vision should set priorities, provide direction and a marker to people to assure that all are able to see whether or not the goals set forth have been achieved.

To create a reliable vision, leaders must first assess and analyses their current situation to get an understanding of where to go. Some steps that are appropriate to take in this stage are considering the evolution of their industry in the future, considering the behaviors of their competitors, and how to innovate successfully to shape their business for competition in the future marketplace. The next step is to undergo some scenario analysis to assess the validity of their vision.

Leadership is, therefore, proactive rather than reactive; looking ahead, problem solving, and constantly evolving.

Once a leader's vision has been developed, it is necessary to sell the vision. In order to do this, he or she has to make the vision compelling and convincing. A compelling vision allows people to understand, embrace, see, and feel it. Effective leaders can communicate their visions effectively and clearly. They are able to speak about their visions in ways that people can relate to and they inform people in an inspired way. This makes people more receptive of their ideas and more inclined to follow what they have to say.

Shared values and vision creation are two major components of leadership. Those who can develop skills in these two areas are more likely to succeed in leadership roles.

*Inspires and motivates people to engage with that vision*

The foundation of leadership is a compelling vision. This vision is only met, however, by a leader's ability to inspire and motivate his or her followers. At the beginning of most projects, it is easier to stay enthusiastic, which in turn makes it easier to win support for it than in other stages of the project. After the initial enthusiasm fades is when it becomes more difficult to maintain an inspiring vision moving forward. People change along with their attitudes and working methods, as well as their goals. Good leadership requires recognizing this phenomenon and working hard throughout a given project to be cognizant of others' needs, hopes, and desires while meeting the vision at hand. It is a juggling act of altruism and pragmatism that helps wherever it goes.

One means of linking effort, motivation, and outcome is known as expectancy theory. This place is an emphasis on leaders linking two main expectations that their followers have. These are listed below:

The expectation of hard work leading to good results.
And
The expectation of good results leading to incentives or rewards.

People with these expectations foresee both intrinsic and extrinsic rewards and therefore work harder to achieve success.

One other approach includes repeatedly restating the vision with added emphasis on its rewards and communicating the vision in a more effective and attractive way.

Expert power is one of the most helpful things that a leader can have. People are more inclined to admire and believe in leaders with this because they are seen as experts at what they do. Expertise comes with credibility, respect, and prestige. This also potentially gives people a right and even an obligation to lead others. Having and displaying competence gives leaders a much easier time motivating and inspiring their followers.

Natural Charisma and appeal can also serve as conduits for a leader's motivation of and influence over people, as well as other sources of power. These other sources of power include the ability to assign tasks to people and to pay bonuses.

*Managing the delivery of the vision*

This area of leadership applies more to management than any of these other tips.

Leaders always need to make sure that they are properly managing the work necessary for delivering their vision. This can be done by either themselves, a manager, or a team of managers delegated by the leader to deliver the vision of the leader.

In order to achieve this, team members need to meet their performance goals linked to the company's vision. Some means of seeing that this is done are KPIs ( key performance indicators), performance management, and project management. One other way of ensuring that the vision is being met is a management style called management by wandering around (MBWA). This style ensures that all the steps that need to be taken are taken in meeting any given goals.

Another trait of an effective leader is the ability to manage change well. Leadership is, after all, constant evolution and adjusting to work's vicissitudes. Managing changes smoothly and efficiently ensures that all goals will be met and obstacles overcome throughout the course of realizing the leader's vision. This can only be done, however, with the backing and support of the people behind the leader.

*Building and coaching a team to achieve the vision*

Some of the more crucial activities carried out by transformational leaders are individual and team development. Without these, there would be nothing for the leader to lead. The first step in developing a team that a leader has to take is to come to understand team dynamics. There are several popular and well-established models that can describe these to leaders, including Belbin's team roles approach, and the forming, storming, norming, performing, and adjourning theory of Bruce Tuckman. A more in depth analysis of this theory is featured below:

*Forming*
The forming step involves a team coming together at the beginning of a venture to figure the goals of the group out and how to go about accomplishing these. Members tend to be impersonal and polite during this period as everyone is still getting oriented within the team.

*Storming*
The storming phase is a bit more selective and critical. In this phase, the leadership may be questioned along with group members ideas. This is very much a culling-off phase of the process as many of the group's members will feel overwhelmed and disconcerted by the turbulence and criticism. Some of them who do not leave after this stage give up on the goal at hand as well. And some just simply do not want to do what is asked of them.

*Norming*
Norming is the step at which the group comes together to agree on a singular plan for achieving the common goal. In this stage, members of the group are encouraged to yield their ideas for the betterment of the group and they also come to know

and understand each other better, building stronger relationships. It is working towards a common goal that brings the team members together.

*Performing*
By the performing stage of the process, the group members are able to work towards accomplishing the goal without very much outside supervision or input. They also come to understand each other's needs better and how to work with one another to accomplish the goal at hand.

*Adjourning*
In the adjourning stage, the opportunity to reflect on unsuccessful and successful outcomes comes about. Members of the group can use these outcomes to gage what they should do when working on future tasks. This will help smooth out the process of meeting a goal in the future.

The next time you find yourself working in a group on a certain task, monitor the group's progress through these stages. Group members tend to move through these stages in all sorts of different orders. They actually rarely happen in the order listed above. If, however, team members are aware of the steps that they are moving through-which they usually are not- then they can typically work through these steps much more efficiently and effectively. Walking yourself through these steps listed above will help you navigate the happenings of your workplace better in the future.

A competent leader always does his or her best to ensure that team members are equipped with all the abilities and skills necessary to do their jobs and achieve the overarching vision. In order to do this, it is necessary to give and receive feedback on a day to day basis, as well as to train and coach team members on a regular basis as well. These steps will improve individual and team performances dramatically.

Good leaders lead, but great leaders lead and find leadership potential. When leading a team, it is always helpful to find leadership abilities on others, whatever their current positions may be. This paves the way for not only differentiation in hierarchical status, but also for further development beyond the leader's influence or even stay. It can also give a leader a surprisingly helpful example in other competent workers.

The terms 'leader' and 'leadership' are often misused to describe people who are actually in managerial positions. These people are often highly skilled and have great work-ethics, but that does not necessarily make them great leaders.

Workplaces are all too often hoisted up on people who others consider to be leaders but are actually managers. These managers often do not provide any aspirations or even long-term goals for their team members, which is fine in the short term, but eventually leads to feelings of meaninglessness and even resentment.

The next discussion points that should be delved into would have to be group dynamics and social engineering. These are important realms to know about when entering a new workplace, or any given social setting for that matter. Here we will look into what group dynamics are and what you need to know about them in order to master them.

Group dynamics, whether ignored by participants or not, play a major role in any culture, organization, or unit. People with differing ideas and perspectives make these groups up. It is very rare that all people and their ideologies are homogeneous within any given group. It is, in fact, also dangerous. Leaders are looked up to within these groups maintain the unity of purpose and cohesiveness of the unit. The cultural bonds within these units must be developed more at certain times than in others. Once these bonds are developed, the further effort has to be put in to nurture them.

Dysfunction within these groups occurs with alienation among specific members. When a member feels ostracized, there is very little keeping him or her from acting out in unpredictable ways. This is bound to come up at times and when it does the leader can struggle to remain objective as the structure of the cohesive unit starts to fall apart. These are usually the worst periods of chaos in the histories of groups. It is these periods, however, that separate good leaders from bad ones.

At all times, if they are understandable or appropriate, the leader or manager must continue to recognize the team member causing the disturbance as an integral part of the group. Further alienation typically leads only to further disturbance. At these times it would be beneficial for the leader to look at the employee causing the disturbance as being a special employee, one who could use the leader's help or skills, one who remains part of the group, and even one who may be there to teach the leader something. A review of the nature of the communication, power, and corporate climate of the unit would also be beneficial under these circumstances in order to further understand the team member's point of view and avoid further disturbances in the future.

A leader must also have abilities in objective introspection. It is not advisable or even possible to guide or help others unless these skills are developed. It is putting the cart before the horse. A leader recognizing his or her own insecurities will be more easily able to perceive and recognize staff dysfunctions as being symptomatic of systematic dysfunctions. The ego will be more open to rationality once personal problems are more specifically addressed. It takes a secure and mature person to decide that staff is ultimately more important than his or her own ideas are moving forward.

Once new steps are taken after dysfunctions much progress can be made and the company can often be left better off than they were beforehand because of this. The staff can find new means of communication and ways to relate to one another, they can find also find new modes of behavior all together that could even boost their self-esteem or overall well-being. Fortunately for the leader, everyone at the company could then boast of having a manager with a plethora of newfound ideas and attitudes. All these intricacies and regulations tend to make working in a group very complicated at times, but if all of these steps are stuck to and everyone pulls their own weight, the benefits of teamwork can be innumerable.

# Conclusion

Thank you for making it through to the end of Dark Psychology. Let's hope this book was as informative and as helpful as possible. We all have a dark side of our psyche whether we admit it or not. Only those who accept and study this dark side can incur the benefits of doing so, and these benefits are some of the greatest we can come across in life, so this book and others like it are some of the greatest resources that we can give ourselves.

Dark psychology could best be described as a study of the human condition in which it becomes normative for people to pray upon others out of criminal and or deviant desires. Often these desires lack specific purpose and are based primarily on basic instinctual desires. Each human has the potential and capacity to victimize other humans, as well as other living creatures, but most of us keep these desires suppressed in order to function successfully in society. Those of us who do not sublimate these dark tendencies are typically representative of the "dark triad": psychopathy, sociopathy, and Machiavellianism, or other mental disorders/psychological disturbances. In this way, dark psychology focuses primarily on the underpinnings (i.e. the thoughts, processing systems, feelings, and behaviors) that are found below the more predatory aspects of our nature, the same ones that go most vigorously against the grain of modern thought concerning human behavior. In this field, we tend to assume that these more abusive, criminal, and deviant behaviors are purposive most of the time, though there are instances in which they seem to have no teleological underpinnings.